VOLUME TWO

A FAITH TO LIVE BY

What an intelligent, compassionate and authentic
21st Century Christian faith looks like

Conversations with Archbishop Justin Welby,
Archbishop Kay Goldsworthy, N.T. Wright, Miroslav Volf,
Stanley Hauwerwas, Jean Vanier, Laurence Freeman, Esther de Waal,
Barry Jones, Tim Costello, Dorothy Lee, Stan Grant and others

Includes a reflection on Pope Francis' spirituality

Edited by

ROLAND ASHBY

Published by Acorn Press
An imprint of Bible Society AustraliaACN 148 058 306
Charity licence 19 000 528
GPO Box 4161
Sydney NSW 2001
Australia
www.acornpress.net.au | www.biblesociety.org.au

© Anglican Media, 2024. All rights reserved.

ISBN 978-0-647-53341-3

First published by Morning Star Publishing in 2018, ISBN 978-0-648-37653-8

Roland Ashby asserts his right under section 193 of the *Copyright Act 1968* (Cth) to be identified as the author of this work.

Apart from any fair dealing for the purposes of private study, research, criticism or review, no part of this work may be reproduced by electronic or other means without the permission of the publisher.

 A catalogue record for this work is available from the National Library of Australia

Editor: Roland Ashby
Cover design: John Healy
Design and typesetting: Ivan Smith

Preface

If Christianity is to continue to be a major force in the world it must be clear in both its message and practice that God is a God of love, compassion and justice who can transform lives. This collection of 31 interviews, and a reflection on Pope Francis' spirituality, which were published in *The Melbourne Anglican* (*TMA*), the award-winning newspaper of the Anglican Diocese of Melbourne, Australia, between 2001 and 2018, present such a vision.

The interviews have been conducted by Roland Ashby, Maggie Fergusson, Emma Halgren, Dr Muriel Porter OAM and the Revd Dr Gordon Preece.

The book provides insights into particular prayer and meditation practices and experiences of the transcendent, and shows how Christianity can be life-giving and life-changing, as well as how the Christian vision can offer hope and wisdom on the great moral issues of our time such as climate change and poverty. It also offers insights into how to understand and dialogue with those of other faiths, particularly Islam.

At a time when faith has been under sustained attack from 'new atheists', it confronts such questions as 'Why does God allow suffering and evil to exist?' while also demonstrating there is a rational and compelling basis for belief.

It also reflects on the future of the Church, and what constitutes effective mission and evangelism.

The book also includes interviews with some leading women in Christian leadership, and how their distinct gifts and experience can help to shape Christianity for the 21st century.

Volume I of *A faith to live by* was published in 2012 by Mosaic Resources (now Morning Star Publishing) in Melbourne, and by Darton, Longman and Todd in the UK.

Roland Ashby has been Editor of *The Melbourne Anglican* (*TMA*) since 1995, holds a Master's degree in theology, and is a Benedictine Oblate.

Foreword

This collection of conversations is founded on the simple proposition that Christians can learn from one another and so deepen their faith.

I warm to the conversational style of the cameos. We are privileged to listen in on deeply personal conversations: intimacy is offered and embraced. We enter places to reflect, pray, learn and act. Through question and answer, unexpected insights are gained into the lives of men and women of faith, and from these flow inspiration, encouragement and challenge to our own following of Christ.

While life's complexities and their over-simplification within the constraints of some social media can feed division and conflict, these interviews allow gentle probing and the drawing out of particularities in the way that faith is exercised.

Rather than differences being divisive, different practices are seen to be enriching: a showing forth of the rich tapestry of God's church, of the Christian faith lived with intelligence, compassion and integrity.

The Editor of this volume, Roland Ashby, has made good use of interviews taken over the years with eminent Christians from around the globe. The conversation partners include scholars, social activists, contemplatives, lay and ordained enriched by participation in religious orders, and lay people integrating faith and work. The variety of the participants and their diverse experiences, motivations and practices provide ample nurture to the reader's faith.

The sense of the presence of the divine in everyday life shaped by rituals, personal and communal, adds to the richness of the experiences shared. We hear of new discoveries and growing appreciations of life in God, of identity and purpose in God's purposes. Here is diversity and depth, insight and practice to enrich our own discipleship. Here also is challenge to evaluate traditions and commitments previously unknown and to grow thereby.

Our diocesan motto, 'Making the Word of God fully known' (from Colossians 1:25) is founded on our own knowing of the Word of God, Jesus Christ. May the Spirit of Christ use this collection of conversations about 21st century Christian faith to deepen our knowing and embolden our making known the Word of God.

The Most Reverend Dr Philip L. Freier
Anglican Archbishop of Melbourne and
Primate of the Anglican Church of Australia

Contents

Alasdair Vance
Benedictine renewal of a psychiatrist's faith 1

Alison Taylor
Taylor-made for bishop through life and faith 7

Andrew Harvey
'Sacred activism' the only way to save the world 11

Barry Jones
Epiphanies, our moral challenges and Trump 19

Bernard McGinn
The power of uniting Mary and Martha 23

Dorothy Lee
Neglect of Spirit impoverishes the faith 27

Esther de Waal
Standing in a place where we can say 'thank you, God'
for all that life holds 31

George Browning
Never forget common good, biblical ethics warn 33

Graham Cole
Sharing a history with God 37

Jean Vanier
How have we loved? In the end it's all that matters 43

Justin Welby
Prayer and suffering 49

Kay Goldsworthy
Church a place of 'grace and healing' despite abuse scandals 53

Kim Nataraja
Religion/spirituality split weakening Christianity 57

Laurence Freeman
Looking death in the face without fear 61

Margaret Harper
Entering into the space and stillness of icons 65

Michael King
Coming face to face with yourself – and God 67

Nigel McCulloch
   Contemplation the key to revival 73

Philip Hughes
   Christendom over, faith enters a new era 77

Ray Simpson & Brent Lyons-Lee
   Call from God leads to global Celtic fellowship 81

Richard Fay
   Healing the 'father wound' in men's psyches 85

Sarah Bachelard
   Letting in the Self that comes to us from God 91

Stan Grant
   'Christianity gave us a divine sense of our equality' 95

Stanley Hauerwas
   The end of Christendom a great opportunity 99

Stephen Cottrell
   Mission not about 'scalp-hunting' for Jesus 103

Steve Bradbury
   Staying close to Jesus calls for a radical generosity to the poor 107

Tim Costello
   An activist for Gospel justice 113

Tom Wright
   Finding the Wright words to tell Bible truths 119
   God came back, in Jesus, to take charge 125
   St Paul's theology often misunderstood 129

Understanding and Engaging with Islam

Dave Andrews
   Violent world needs the 'Jihad' of Jesus 135

John Azumah
   Battle for the soul of Islam underway 139

Miroslav Volf
   Embracing the 'other' in love, truth and grace 145
   Christianity marginalised if new media ignored 151

William T. Cavanaugh
   Church called to go out onto the 'field of battle' 155

Appendix
   Understanding Pope Francis' spirituality 159

Benedictine renewal of a psychiatrist's faith

Professor Alasdair Vance is Academic Head of Child Psychiatry at the University of Melbourne, Australia. He talks to Roland Ashby about the value of meditation for children and his own calling to follow a more contemplative path. The interview appeared in the December 2007 edition of *TMA*.

RA: You have said that the fostering of deep thinking and contemplation is the way to protect our children from our rapidly changing, media-driven, consumer-driven, technology-driven culture. Catholic schools in the Northern Territory are now teaching meditation to children – something like 1500 teachers have been taught how to meditate and how to teach meditation. What do think of meditation for children, and why are you promoting contemplation?

AV: I think that meditation for children is an excellent way forward because children need some balance in their educational lives – academically, in the classroom, as well as socially, in the playground. And meditation can help them work toward that balance. Working toward that balance is critical because children have to develop these self-reflective capacities themselves, they can't have these given to them on a platter. They have to expand their internal horizons as well as their external horizons. I think that in our culture, because change has become almost one of the only constants, it's very hard to develop those internal horizons. Meditation is actually a technique than can help achieve this.

RA: Can you expand on that in terms of how you understand meditation spiritually? What do you believe is going on?

AV: Well, I am a very committed disciple of Christ, so I can only answer that question about what is occurring spiritually from my own context as a committed Christian. I believe that the Holy Spirit is experienced and evident through meditation. I believe in the spiritual realm, that human beings are becoming more aware and open to the experience of a living relationship with the living God through the Holy Spirit here on earth.

I believe that meditation can offer a conduit and an openness to that experience that is very personal and therefore very healing and re-creative and developing for the person. I think that the Holy Spirit is experienced in and underpins the whole of the creation, so I'm not saying that the personal experience of God through meditation is the only way one experiences God through the Holy Spirit, but it is the most personal way.

There are many other important offshoots though. One of the most important is that meditation involves an acute, sensitive awareness to the internal world, and that acute sensitive awareness can very much involve optimal brain and mind function within a place of great, acute awareness and internal balance. People often think that meditation is akin to going to sleep; it's quite the opposite, as Thomas Merton popularised through the contemplative monastic movement. Meditation is very active.

RA: Can you give us some idea of your own meditation life? How do you meditate?

AV: Again I have to answer that question by being clear that I experienced quite a profound call from God to a contemplative life about 18 months to two years ago. It was not something that I chose, but in obedience to God's call on my life. I operate within a Benedictine model – Benedict's rule for life – and I have a Morning and Evening Office that I pray, as well as an ongoing use of the Jesus prayer ('Lord Jesus, Son of God, have mercy on me a sinner') throughout the day as the basis of my meditative practice. In other words, there is a rhythm for me in the morning and evening office as well as the Jesus prayer, that helps me to reorient my life constantly to my personal experience of the Holy Spirit. Through these practices resonances begin to emerge throughout the whole of my life, as I begin to work toward being in a state of constant prayer, constant openness to the Holy Spirit, no matter how busy I am at the university or in the hospital.

RA: Could you say a little bit more about the call that you received, or is that too personal?

AV: No, nothing's too personal. As a disciple of Christ I'm very happy to share with you, and if my own experience can be helpful that's a good thing. I believe that as a middle-aged man I was at some level stuck in a rather intellectualised, rigid and barren form of faith for many years. I had grown up with strong social justice leanings, the need to "do good" and to extend God's kingdom here on earth through powerfully working with others to do good. But intellectually I was very influenced by much of the liberal protestant German theology and I unfortunately developed a cynical view of questions of personal engagement with God. And God just washed that away, really.

The call was quite a dramatic turn for me. I was not naturally moving toward this, I really just got moved out of my rather barren intellectual context I was in. I saw a Benedictine breviary in a second hand bookshop and thought it looked interesting so I bought it. I then read it and thought, my goodness, these prayers and psalms are wonderful – and I began to pray it. I then felt drawn to ring up the Anglican Benedictine abbey at Camperdown… and I've been becoming an oblate ever since.

RA: So in addition to the Benedictine rhythm of prayer that you're now following, what other aspects of the Benedictine tradition are you trying to integrate into your life?

AV: I've been profoundly moved by the importance of understanding that Alasdair Vance as a disciple of Jesus can only fully become Alasdair Vance through being in community and through focussing on the community fully achieving its potential. In other words, the individual can only fully become who they are meant to be, can only fully reach their potential, through others also reaching their potential. So there is a profound selflessness in becoming fully a person. That's been a profound influence for me, because it's made me realise that although I sometimes have trouble, being quite an introvert, finding the energy to relate to a lot of people, people and all the creation are profoundly important, and I have to work toward the whole creation becoming fully what it can be in God.

That has led me to a very strong relational theology and I often think about the Middle Age icons that focus on the community of God, particularly the famous one by Rublev, because I see the creation as actually an extension of that community, and that my role is to work with people like you Roland and others, brothers and sisters, to extend God's kingdom here on earth for all our sakes. I think that's a very powerful Benedictine model and that St Benedict through his rule helped people achieve that practically, and that's why it's had such an ongoing legitimacy. It's not part of a particular club, football team, whether catholic or evangelical, or whatever; it's part of a way of discipleship than can allow people to achieve that end.

I think finally that Benedictine thinking has helped me understand that I'm drawn into that community of God, and I find that my own habits, my own ways of being have been transformed. God really does chisel away at me; and in all my gross imperfections I'm becoming a better husband, a better father, a better member of the community, whereas before I was in a rather cynical intellectual and rather dry position – sometimes full of hate. I think I'm much more full of love now than before, when I think I gave more attention to my hates and to the things I didn't like. Almost like the cup was always half empty, there were always problems, rather than seeing the goodness and the outflow of that goodness through the community of God.

RA: Are there tensions between your religious beliefs and practice and your scientific beliefs and practice, or do you see them as complementary?

AV: I think at one point I saw them as complementary, but I think that's false – there are great tensions. I think these are fundamentally different discourses, and I've come to the view now, as a clinical scientist and as a middle-aged man, that scientific discourse is fundamentally a mechanistic discourse that seeks to define and control confounding variables. So you set up experiments in order to determine associations given the fact that you've controlled all these other elements.

The faith discourse is completely separate. It is a discourse that is built on the mystical, and at its heart is built on this living relationship with God. My role as a Christian is to follow Christ's call, to pick up the cross that he gives me and to take on those tasks that he gives me; whether I like it or not – that's immaterial. What's important is the relationship, and the structures of the church help me have that relationship and experience that relationship in community. That faith-based discourse is not scientific; it is spiritual, it is wholly me as a human being responding in my totality to the living God. Now of course, there are going to be elements of that faith experience that one can study scientifically, but the discourses are fundamentally separate. And there can be great tensions.

The most significant tension currently is the whole development of cloning technologies and the ability to reproduce and manipulate the very building blocks of life. As a scientist I think these are wonderful, exciting tools to play with, to creatively understand and work out. But the mystical discourse, the spiritual discourse, the wisdom that the Church seeks to transmit as the kingdom of God extended here on earth, would point out the dangers of playing with tools that we do not fully understand. I think that is a great tension, and I, as a disciple of Christ, feel a great sense of unease about the problem of quite profound ethical questions not being adequately addressed as the techniques, the tools of science and the play of science gather pace – such as the recent cloning of a non-human primate.

RA: In terms of the discipline of psychology, there'd be a number of critics of religion, wouldn't there? Freud, obviously, in terms of religion being an expression of dependency on some kind of father figure, and also the Feuerbach critique that it's all basically wishful thinking. How do you reconcile your faith to some of that?

AV: I think those criticisms are quite bereft. They're criticisms by people who do not understand the mystical and the power of metaphor, the power of love and relationships of love that have transformed our world.

It is no accident to me that Benedictine thinking actually held the light, kept the candle going, through the darkest times of a divided, fragmented Dark Ages Europe. It is no surprise to me that some of the great icons of our age, such as Mother Teresa, were very faithful disciples of Jesus and followed his call; and that even today, at the very heart of the church, countless brothers and sisters, men and women, children and young people are following Jesus' call into a very deep personal relationship that motivates their love, which is at the very heart of the community of God's expression in the creation.

It is an act of love, and the psychology that talks about wish fulfilment is rather tawdry in the light of very powerful lived examples. This young man in his early 30s who was nailed to a cross was not operating according to some tawdry, rather trite intellectual abstraction. It was manifest love, and it motivates my life. And that's all that counts! In other words, an intellectual idea is meaningless in the light of that expression of God's love. That is everything.

RA: I'm also interested in the difference between the mind and soul. It's very noticeable if somebody suffers brain damage, or somebody has dementia, that their whole personality and identity change considerably. So it seems that there is an obvious connection between the mind and the soul and a person's spirit. Do you accept that, or do you argue that somebody with advanced dementia for example is perhaps less human than a person with his or her full faculties?

AV: It's an excellent question and a profound one. My immediate answer would be as follows. My understanding of God's relationship with the creation is truly panentheistic, that God is both within and outside of creation but supporting it; and I also believe in this construct of theosis – that through our personal relationship and our discipleship with Jesus we are being transformed. And that has biological, psychological, social and spiritual elements – it is holistic, God operates across the lot.

I think therefore the transfiguration of Christ also for me has a physical element. So I have no problems whatsoever with the view that the spiritual, the soul, the mind and the brain are all equally important and part of a human being, and have to be valued, which is why we need theological discourse along with philosophical, psychological and biological discourses. We can't do without any of those, but we privilege one over the other at our peril if the question that we're being asked to address involves one or more of those elements. If we exclude them, we're not answering the question. I think the person with dementia is a person who has a brain pathology that affects their mind. I think it would be a very brave person who would say that their soul is affected, because in that spiritual realm we are all equal at the foot of the cross. We are all equally important disciples of Jesus.

RA: And finally I'm interested in how you understand, as a scientist, what's going on in prayer and meditation in terms of brain activity, and how you measure those higher levels of consciousness.

AV: Fascinating question. The answer is there's no doubt that the thalamus, which is a key central organising, integrating area of the brain, is more active during meditation. There's been some wonderful research with some monks and nuns who have allowed their brains to be scanned while they're meditating. And there's no doubt that there are key areas of the brain linked to the thalamus that are much more active in the meditation state. This is not surprising – meditation is a very active process of becoming aware of much deeper rhythms and experiences and higher and more intense levels of consciousness.

Taylor-made for bishop through life and faith

Alison Taylor became Australia's fourth woman bishop in April 2013. She spoke to Muriel Porter for the May 2013 edition of *TMA*.

Giving birth to her first child is always a major turning point in the life of any woman. For Alison Taylor, the birth of her daughter Miranda was particularly significant. Having a baby released her vocation to ordained ministry, she told *TMA*. "Once I had a child, I could truly be myself," she said.

Until that happy day, the childlessness of the previous 17 years of her marriage had consumed her, she explained. Having suffered several miscarriages, she had to spend a great deal of time resting in hospital during her successful pregnancy. No wonder Miranda's name was chosen because it means "to be marvelled at", or "miracle".

"I felt as if I had been shot out of a cannon," she said. "I had responded to childlessness by working harder and harder; now I could be myself."

So in 1993 – the year after the first women priests were ordained in Australia – Bishop Taylor began theological study at Melbourne's Trinity College Theological School, where she gained first class honours in systematic theology.

She was ordained in 1997, and began the journey of parish, school and archidiaconal ministry that led to her consecration as a bishop in St John's Cathedral, Brisbane, on 6 April 2013. She is now bishop for Brisbane Diocese's southern region.

Before her life turned around so dramatically, Bishop Taylor had been a highly successful town planner. She had been variously deputy director (conservation) of the National Trust of Australia (Victoria), senior lecturer in urban studies at Victoria University of Technology, and a part-time member of what is now the Victorian Civil and Administrative Tribunal. She had also, with newborn Miranda in tow, been director of the Tianjin Urban Conservation Project in China, a project of the Australian International Development Assistance Board (now AUSAID).

She had been an active member of her parish, St Mary's, North Melbourne, serving as Vestry member and churchwarden.

"Vicars who have been churchwardens understand the realities of parish life," she commented. "They know that lay people are not just there to keep things going and arrange the flowers. They understand that lay people have a serious ministry in their own right."

Sydney-born, she had grown up an Anglican, spending her early childhood years at St Alban's, Lindfield, before her family's move to Melbourne. St Mark's, Camberwell became her parish, where she was confirmed and taught Sunday school.

But a stage of alienation from the church followed. During her time at university she was angry that the church was not speaking out against the Vietnam War.

It was the "bottomless pit" of childlessness that eventually drew her back to the church, this time to St Mary's, North Melbourne, where a stellar clutch of clergy and lay people were gathered. It quickly became her spiritual home.

She was able to assist the parish materially through her planning and conservation work, helping the parish access a $40,000 grant from the Historic Buildings Council to undertake vital roof repairs. It was a great deal of money in the early '90s. At the time she was using her husband's surname – Blake – so the grant quickly became known as the "Blake Prize for Church Restoration"!

Following ordination, Bishop Taylor was jointly curate at St John's, Malvern, and chaplain at Korowa Anglican Girls' School, before becoming curate at St John's, Toorak.

Her first role as vicar was at St Dunstan's, Camberwell, where she was also appointed Archdeacon of Kew.

She moved to St John's, Camberwell in 2010.

Relinquishing the territorial archdeacon position last year, she had just become Archdeacon of International Partnerships for the Diocese when she received the call to the episcopate. This role had reflected her involvement, at the personal invitation of the Archbishop of Canterbury, in the steering group for the international Anglican Alliance for Development Relief and Advocacy.

Overseas aid has been a longstanding passion of Bishop Taylor's. She was Chair of Anglican Overseas Aid (formerly Anglicord) from 2005 until her move to Brisbane, having served on the agency's board since 2001. Her work in China in the early 1990s was another aspect of this interest.

Her aid activism has been a key factor in her interest in Ignatian spirituality.

"I was looking for a spirituality that really spoke to my activist side," she explained.

In 2005, she undertook a 30-week retreat in daily life through the Campion Centre of Ignatian Spirituality, Kew. The program, an adaptation of the traditional 30-day Ignatian full-time retreat, involves intensive Scripture reading and a weekly meeting with a spiritual director.

The 16th century founder of the Jesuits, St Ignatius of Loyola, lived at a time when virtually everyone believed in God and in Jesus, but many did not really have a relationship with, or connection to, God, she explained. He developed spiritual exercises designed to build that relationship, and help people come closer to God. They are, she said, a "great treasure for the church".

"He emphasised the value of the imagination, so you use your imagination to enter into biblical passages to encounter God there. They are primarily Gospel-based. Ignatius emphasised that we are co-workers with Christ in the world, and this was important for my desire to work in overseas aid. This is a spirituality that has really worked for me."

As a pioneer woman leader in the church, Bishop Taylor notes that it is hard to do what you have not seen modelled. There are clearly few models for women bishops, but the same is still true for women clergy. Not many new women clergy have worked in parishes where the vicar is a woman, for instance. She is also concerned that women clergy are not mentoring young women enough. By comparison, there seems to be plentiful mentoring for young men, she said.

She is concerned, too, about the church's continuing reluctance to change. Her experience as a town planner and academic, and her marriage to Trevor Blake, a senior Victorian public servant, have shown her that the public service and the business world are these days determined to be as efficient and as progressive as they can be.

"The church is the only body that still wants to continue doing what it has always done. Its conservatism is not related to tradition properly understood, or to Scripture. There is a real tension all the time between staying as you are, and changing. That is something every vicar has to deal with."

That tension is graphically focused in a bishop who is a woman in a church where bishops are overwhelmingly male, and where they are likely to remain mostly male perhaps for decades to come.

The church in 2013 is more like the bifurcated world in which she began her professional life nearly 40 years ago. In the first university department in which she worked, the gender divide was stark, with almost all the academics male while the administrative staff was female. Young emerging female academics were not encouraged as their male counterparts were.

That world had changed dramatically by the time Alison began theological study in the 1990s.

"I felt I had stepped back in time to the 1970s," she said.

The assumption in the church was still that men would take the public role, while women would look after the private area of life, caring for children and the sick.

She freely admits she is "not so good at the private role". Rather, her extensive background as a professional woman offering significant leadership in the community has prepared her well to offer an important role model for the public leadership of women in the 21st century church.

....

Dr Muriel Porter OAM, a journalist, church historian, and author of several books on contemporary Australian Anglicanism, has been a member of the Australian General Synod for the past 30 years. In her parish, she is an authorised lay preacher and cantor.

See 'Understanding Pope Francis' spirituality' in the Appendix.

'Sacred activism' the only way to save the world

If the world is to be saved then human consciousness must undergo a radical transformation, argues Indian-born author, teacher and mystic Andrew Harvey. He spoke to Roland Ashby for the December 2013 edition of *TMA*.

RA: You believe the human race and the planet have reached a point of great danger. You talk about this time as being a tragic and terrible moment of our evolutionary history and that we're in the throes of a great battle. What do you see as terrible and tragic, and what is the battle?

AH: Well, it's quite clear, I think, that we have reached a point at which all of the projects, agendas and fantasies that we've spun out of our collective false self are now totally bankrupt. It's quite clear that our culture in its desperate pursuit of domination and exploitation of nature and its addiction to greed, has reached a point where it's not only destroying our world, but also destroying us inwardly. There is a soullessness, a meaninglessness, an apathy, a paralysis, which are as dangerous as the crisis itself.

But I think my work is dedicated not just to waking people up to the extent of the crisis, but to waking people up to the opportunity presented by this crisis. A very great crisis is also a very great opportunity, and what I've come to understand from my own innermost experience and from the true mystical traditions, is that what we are living through is nothing less than a global dark night. What happens in the dark night is that the false self is systematically and ruthlessly destroyed, and an opportunity created for a wholly new relationship with reality and entry into divine consciousness.

So I think of this as an evolutionary crisis in which humanity will have to face the destructiveness of all of its shadows and its false self, but I think it also has a tremendous evolutionary opportunity. Because if we can face this, if we can evolve new ways of being and doing everything – and I believe we can – then a wholly new kind of human being will be born, and a wholly new human race will be engendered. That's what my work is dedicated to: waking people up so that they can go through the process that will empower them to birth the divine in the human and start co-creating with God, a new world.

RA: You've called this waking up process sacred activism. How do you define it?

AH: I have two fundamental definitions of sacred activism. One is user-friendly and for the media: when you combine deep spirituality, deep understanding and reverence for the sacred in life and the sacred in the creation with urgent, wise, focused action, you birth a holy force that can transform everything. We've seen this holy force in the 20th century, for example in Gandhi's slow patient overturning of the British Empire; in the extraordinary heroism of Martin Luther King and his avoidance of a massive bloodbath in race relations; and in Desmond Tutu's and Nelson Mandela's heroic desire to bring in reconciliation and forgiveness as a way of healing the wounds between white and black in South Africa.

The good news is that if you bring together the best of the mystic with the best of the activist, the fire of the mystic's passion for God with the fire of activist's passion for justice, you create a third fire, which is the fire of love and wisdom and action with which, I think, if the human race allows itself to be inspired by this, an enormous revolution can take place.

That brings me to my second definition of sacred activism which is more esoteric and more profound. If these two fires come together: the fire of the passion for God, and the fire of the passion for justice, the third fire that they engender is a quantum leap in power, in energy, in passion. I believe that third fire is actually the evolutionary love fire of the Godhead that created the universe, erupted in the Big Bang, lives as the secret divine presence in everything, and is the evolutionary urge behind the whole unfolding of the universe.

So I believe that sacred activism is, in its deepest sense, the birthing power, the birthing fire, the birthing passion of a new divine humanity, and that the crisis is actually a crisis designed by God, designed by the evolutionary urge of the universe to force humanity to transform or die out.

But the transformation that's required now is not a transformation just into divine consciousness; it's a transformation into divine consciousness in action, and this is where the example of Jesus is so important. I think what

Jesus truly came to do was to open up an evolutionary path, and that path is the path of passionate divine love and profound divine wisdom in action, a path that now hundreds of millions, if not billions of human beings, need to take to help the divine birth out of this chaos, out of this dark night, a wholly new kind of humanity and life on earth.

RA: In *Radical Passion – Sacred Love and Wisdom in Action* you say this is essentially the message of the parable of the prodigal son.

AH: I think the prodigal son is in a way the evolutionary map of humanity. You have the son who gets high on himself, goes and wastes all of his powers in greed, in lust, in self-absorption, in the terrible narcissism that afflicts our culture, and burns totally out, realises that none of these things are going to work. And in desperation and heartbreak, he goes back to the source, back to the father, who is also a mother, and finds not only is he not going to be punished but that his experience has hollowed him out so he is able to receive the true grace, the true generosity of the mercy of God.

That I think is where we are at; we're at that moment of realising that all of our gains, fantasies and agenda are bankrupt, and that there is only one thing that can help us go forward, and that is divine grace, divine energy, divine passion. But the beauty of the nature of the divine is that that is perpetually offered to us. That's why I believe sacred activism is the key to the transformation of the world.

RA: In *Radical Passion* you write that Christ's most devastating weapon in the war of love was his humility.

AH: I think that the most shattering thing about Jesus is that he was clearly imbued with every kind of divine power, but he never used this power to glamourise himself or make himself special. He was actually saying to the human race, 'Don't you understand, you have divine consciousness? Don't you understand that if only you could do the work of opening to that divine consciousness, you would be empowered with just the powers that I have, and that together, we could co-create a wholly new world.' This is Jesus' essential message.

You see this humility throughout his ministry. When he healed people, he nearly always said to them, 'It is your faith that has made you whole; it's not my powers alone.' You can see this humility in the way in which he says to his disciples, 'You're not servants but friends. You're not in a subsidiary hierarchical relationship to me. You're my friends. I love you. Let's do this together.'

Above all, you can see it in the Last Supper when he dresses up as a female servant, which is the lowest of the low in terms of his society, and washes the feet of his disciples in one last desperate attempt to stop them projecting onto him the glory that he was trying to give to them.

One of the great testimonies of the Christian mystical tradition is that if only you can truly believe in what Jesus is saying, that we all have divine consciousness, and with God can do extraordinary things in the name of God, extraordinary feats of healing and courage, then everything could be changed.

The essential way of Jesus is the way of radical humility, of radical service to all beings, and that is what has to be kept at the core of the enacting of the Christ consciousness, because if we don't have that humility, that reverence before the whole of life and before all beings, we will never be able to be empty enough to be continually receiving the grace to be able to give the kind of help that we need to give.

RA: You obviously see Jesus as a mystic, but this is not how he is commonly understood.

AH: Jesus is certainly the greatest mystic of humanity, but he realised the essential role of mysticism, which is not to provide endless entertainment for the psyche, but to provide the foundation of divine consciousness, divine courage, divine understanding, that would give you the chutzpah, the passion to set about doing God's work in the world, and God's work in the world is very clear. God's work is the transformation of all of the institutions and arts and sciences of this world into a living representation of divine love and divine justice.

So Jesus is delivering a tremendous slap in the face to all of the mystical traditions that are escapist, narcissistic and addicted to transcendence. He is also delivering a very, very strong slap to the face of activists who believe that they could change the world simply out of righteous anger. That's not going to be enough. You're going to have to have a foundation in divine consciousness, and an openness to divine grace, otherwise your actions will not be widely inspired enough and not go far enough.

Jesus' whole life is an example of what a true mystical life really is: it isn't about only getting in connection with the divine; it's about getting so deeply in connection with the divine that you marry the two sides of the divine nature in yourself – the very great peace of knowing that you are in divine consciousness, and the very great passion of the mother side of the divine to see that every being is protected and that justice is done on every level, and that compassionate harmony is lived out, not only with human beings but with the whole creation.

Jesus is the supreme mystical revolutionary of history, and it's only when humanity – all of humanity, not just Christians – really takes seriously this enormous fusion that happened in Jesus between transcendent and immanent, mother and father, body and soul, heart and mind, deep, deep prayer and inner mystical practice with very clear, wise, fierce radical action, that we will be able to go forward. Jesus is really the key, I think, to the future of human evolution, just as he has been the key to the real relationship with God.

RA: And his spirit is available to us all through the Cosmic Christ. Can you say something about how you understand the term, 'the cosmic Christ'?

AH: In all of the great mystical traditions, there has been a revelation of the universe as fundamentally having two aspects, and of the divine as having two aspects: an impersonal aspect, in which the laws of divine consciousness are worked out on every level; and even more mysteriously, a personal aspect in which the divine can be contacted as a sublime universal person who cares enormously deeply for every single being out of the mystery of total love. This marriage of the impersonal and the personal is found in every tradition.

In the Christian tradition, this is known as the Cosmic Christ. And the Cosmic Christ is the great universal creative love force of the universe that is also a mysterious being who is totally in love with each one of his creations, and is able to turn to each one creation with infinite care. Jesus lived the life of the Cosmic Christ on the earth; he showed its passion, its radicalism, its nakedness, its vulnerability, its almost insane love for everyone. And in living that life on the earth, he attained total identification with this impersonal person, and in the Resurrection, he birthed himself into that universal love force, and now he is the personal face of that universal love force.

Jesus is completely alive, both as the impersonal divine and as this shatteringly naked, vulnerable, amazingly beautiful holy person, so that if you awaken to him in devotion, you can have a deeply personal relationship with him.

RA: In *Son of Man – the mystical path to Christ*, you describe the four stages of the Christ path.

AH: The traditional Christian mystical path has had three stages, and they're very profound: purgation, illumination and union. What I have done in *Son of Man* is to extend that, because it's not enough. In the first stage, purgation, which I call awakening, what happens is that you awaken to your divine consciousness, and through revelation and through deep sacred discipline, you are directly more and more empowered with it.

The second stage, 'illumination', is when these powers possess you and inform you and infuse you, and your mind and heart are immeasurably expanded, and you begin the mystery of theosis, the mystery of divine light coming down into the body. There is a great danger at this stage of the path, and that is that you appropriate these powers for your subtle ego, and that's why at the end of illumination, what occurs is that the mystic goes through the equivalent of the crucifixion in terms of their own nature, the dark night that strips them of the last vestiges of their subtle ego, so that the much vaster transcendent immanent consciousness of the Cosmic Christ can be born in them without interference from the ego.

And then you enter the third part of the path, which is union. But in *Son of Man*, I've extended this vision of union to show us that union doesn't just mean union with divine consciousness in the mind and the heart and the soul, it also means the progressive cellular transformation of the body, and this is very important because what happens in this third stage, I believe, is that the enormous radioactive power that was released by the Resurrection is experienced directly by the mystic, and that the human being is born as a human divine being in which the mind is illuminated, the heart is expanded and the body is subtly transformed.

And this leads to the fourth stage, which I think is absolutely essential for Christians to get real about, because it is what we see so nakedly and wonderfully in the life of Jesus, and this is what I call 'birthing'. What union makes you is a mother/father of divine works, of divine justice, of divine outpouring of those powers to transform this world into the kingdom/queendom.

The tragedy of much conventional Christian mysticism has been its other-worldliness. Jesus wasn't other-worldly at all. He was absolutely focused on all of the tragic problems of the growing patriarchy of his time, on the treatment of women, on the claim of the priest to mediate divine reality instead of empowering people, the appalling selfishness of the rich.

It's very important that the great powers that are experienced along this journey do not become dedicated just to the individual salvation of the person, but dedicated as Jesus dedicated them to the transformation of society. So in birthing in the fourth stage, you become like St Francis, St Teresa of Avila or Hildegard of Bingen, or like any of the great Christed beings. You become revolutionaries of love, overturning the hierarchies and elites of your time by bringing in a wholly new divine energy and a wholly new, transformatory vision of divine justice.

RA: In *Son of Man* you write that an essential foundation for the four stages is a serious spiritual practice.

AH: It would be very difficult to understand anything I've been saying without making a serious daily spiritual practice a priority.

Prayer in all its forms is essential, as is the practice of 'cool' and 'hot' practices.

'Cool' practices such as meditation using a mantra, as in the Jesus Prayer, Centering Prayer and John Main traditions initiate us into the great radiant peaceful awareness that is divine awareness, the peace that passes all understanding.

'Hot' practices include the Sacred Heart tradition as practised by St Mary Margaret Alacoque, or meditation on Jesus' Passion as practised by St Teresa of Avila.

By connecting with Jesus' passion in this way your heart is opened up immensely to the 'insanity' of love that's streaming towards the human race through Jesus and the Cosmic Christ, and from which you can find unbelievable reserves of courage and fortitude.

RA: That expression, 'the insanity of love', reminds me of the 13th century Franciscan poet Jacopone da Todi who writes about the 'frenzy of love' God has for us in his poem 'How the soul through the senses finds God in all creatures', which you have included in your book *The Essential Mystics*.

AH: I think he is one of the great undiscovered mystical poets of Christianity, largely because in his youth he refused God in profligate living, had a conversion experience, and then slowly found his way through, like the prodigal son, to an embrace by the father.

His extraordinary poem begins,
Oh love, divine love,
why do you lay siege to me?
in a frenzy of love for me,
you find no rest.

And he goes through the different ways in which love reaches out to us through our senses, in hearing, sight, taste, touch and smell, and that hiding from this love is impossible. The poem is an expression of how deeply we want to experience divine love, but also how deeply we resist it.

It powerfully describes the dilemma that we all face when we come into contact with this love:
Love, I flee from You,
afraid to give You my heart,
I see that You make me
one with You,
I cease to be me and can no longer find myself

Divine love is going to devour the ego and the ego is terrified. But there is something that really tempts us out of that dilemma, and that for a Christian is obviously Jesus, because Jesus is inescapable once you turn to him. He will devour you. The Flemish 14th century mystic Ruusbroec says that 'Jesus' love is a bulimic love', that it will eat you alive.

Anybody who has the experience of loving Jesus will know that even beginning to love him in a haphazard and very self-absorbed way will break you slowly into the radiant 'insanity' of the love that possesses him and drives him to give everything, absolutely everything, for the transformation of the human race, including submitting himself to the most horrible torture and horror of the death of the crucifixion.

And however hard you try to escape the beauty and holiness and amazing power of that love, one fine day it will get you and you will have to turn towards it, you will have to try, with all of your limitations and follies, to mirror it in your own life. That's what makes Jesus so dangerous. And thank God he is that dangerous because it's only somebody that dangerous that can wake us out of our terminal narcissism.

Barry Jones on epiphanies, our moral challenges and Trump

Australian national living treasure and polymath Dr Barry Jones AC talks to Roland Ashby about his powerful experience of the transcendent and why he finds a divine order compelling. The interview appeared in the June 2017 edition of *TMA*.

Barry Jones describes himself as a "Northern Hemisphere Christian". "If I go to Europe, almost the first thing I'll do is make a beeline for a cathedral, particularly if there's religious music on. I've had so many numinous experiences in some of the great European cathedrals that it's a very special part of fulfilling myself."

A former minister for science in the Hawke Government, and the only member of all four of Australia's academies of science, humanities, social science, and technology and engineering, Dr Jones says he is a life-long sufferer of "Stendhal's Syndrome", the experience of being completely overwhelmed, physically and emotionally, in the presence of transcendent beauty.

In his memoir, *A Thinking Reed*, he writes: "I recognise the numinous when I encounter it, responding by a shuddering in my spine, changed breathing, faster heartbeat, heightened emotion, the lightning strike of imagination, an unexpected sense of familiarity with something completely unknown, places, sights and sounds which transcend the normal and quotidian."

He goes on to describe two powerful numinous experiences or epiphanies he had on his sixtieth birthday. "One was in the great octagonal Palatine Chapel of Aachen Cathedral, consecrated in 805, built for the Emperor Charlemagne in Romanesque style and inspired by his visits to St Vitale in Ravenna, very simple but with some Eastern features, including alternating black and white stones in the arches.

"I felt an overwhelming need to pray, coupled with an out-of-body experience which I cannot rationalise or even explain coherently, except as a brief moment of rapture or possession."

The second epiphany occurred, he writes, "in the nearby town of Trier, in the Gothic church of St Gangolf in the market square. I walked in to the empty church to hear an organist practising, over and over, Bach's *Prelude and Fugue in E Minor,* BWV 548, one of his supreme achievements. I felt overwhelmed, and the structure, logic and irresistible power of the music compelled a sense of divine order."

Bach, he told *TMA*, had an "extraordinary intelligence, operating at a kind of incandescent level. There is something absolutely elemental and universal about him."

He agrees that something of the same divine order Bach's music points to can be discerned in the laws of mathematics, citing the book *Just Six Numbers*, by Martin Rees. "It's a remarkable book. I don't think Rees accepts the God hypothesis, but he does say there appear to be immutable laws that are strange. You have to have these very fine tolerances otherwise the system simply doesn't work. If the force of gravity is too strong or too weak, everything would go wrong. If temperatures are outside a particular kind of tolerable range, life would be impossible."

In terms of religious belief, among writers, two Frenchmen, Montaigne and Pascal, have been the most influential in his life. Montaigne warned of the dangers of dogmatism and fundamentalism, and Pascal had an intense and life-changing religious experience, which he recorded in a note he sewed into his coat: "Fire. God of Abraham, God of Isaac, God of Jacob, not of the philosophers and the scholars...

I will not forget thy word. Amen."

Pascal also famously said: "All mankind's unhappiness derives from one thing: his inability to know how to remain in repose in one room."

Dr Jones agrees that "many people are very uncomfortable with themselves". "Montaigne puts very heavy emphasis on getting to know yourself and devoting time to yourself. He also memorably said that we all need to maintain 'a little room at the back of the shop' where you retreat to and no one else is there." In other words, a contemplative space, where, Dr Jones says, "you've got no iPhone, no computer, no people, but you might have some books. You just develop yourself. It's very important you find that space."

Even, I suggest, for Presidents of the United States?

"Don't get me started on that. One of the most worrying and detestable things about Donald Trump is his complete lack of curiosity. He has no intellectual curiosity at all. He either knows the answer already irrespective of what the question is or he doesn't need to be told, or he will only look for what reinforces the way he feels and that he, not the subject, is central to everything. It's how he feels, how he reacts. That really is the mindset of the toddler."

Dr Jones, who was at one time a lay preacher in the Methodist Church, says his interest in religion was kindled, not by his parents, who weren't religious, but by a grandmother who was devout and to whom he was particularly close, and whose father had had a conversion experience. He has read the Bible from cover to cover three times; the Beatitudes and Corinthians 13:1-13 are among his favourite verses; and he describes Jesus as a "uniquely powerful and charismatic teacher". "Jesus was open and not dogmatic... But I'm horrified, and I'd like to think he'd be horrified, about how he's been used as kind of a back-up force for rather authoritarian rigidity: 'You must believe along these lines and there's no other way things can be handled.' I find that very disconcerting."

Among Christian art the two paintings that have had the most profound impact on him are *The Crucifixion* from the Issenheim Altarpiece by Matthias Grünewald, and *The Resurrection* by Piero della Francesca.

"I'm not sure you can find adequate words to really explain the Grünewald Crucifixion... But it captures the profundity of what happened to Jesus and the universality of it: the crucifixion of mankind, the cruelty of torture and the destruction of every kind of dignity that we find in repressive regimes all over the world.

"Piero della Francesca's *Resurrection* is also extraordinary, described by some, including Aldous Huxley, as the greatest painting ever made. I was over 80 when I got to see it, but I recommend you see it when you're young and active because it's absolutely magical."

Does he agree with Kevin Rudd that climate change is the great moral issue of our time?

"Yes; that and refugees. In the early period of his prime ministership, I was perhaps closer to Rudd than I am now, but I was eager to encourage him to take action because it was a classic illustration of where you had to act in a way that may inhibit current patterns of consumption, because of the need to conserve the environment and preserve it for a future generation. In the end, the politics just went pear-shaped and he decided nothing could be done about it at that stage. This was a tragedy, for practical purposes. I think the environment has essentially been off the political agenda, it hasn't been a priority area, for the last decade, and I think we will come to regret that decision bitterly.

"But the treatment of refugees is also appalling. And it's appalling because in part, you've got the fallacy of the false antithesis, that you say, look, there are only two alternatives: they either drown at sea in leaky boats, or we lock them up and make sure the guards bash them up from time to time. They're the only two alternatives.

"Well they're not! Part of the problem is the failure of both political parties, I think, to do any kind of comprehensive analysis, a statistical analysis. I mean in Europe they're dealing with a refugee problem in terms of millions, perhaps tens of millions. We're dealing with thousands, perhaps even tens of thousands. It is a manageable problem.

"It seems to me absolutely despicable. You see, once you reach bipartisanship, or at least effective bipartisanship, that means there's no room for debate.

"The public opinion polls have said yes, bashing up refugees is quite popular so why would you challenge that? So I'm just dismayed by the whole political process at the moment over that issue because of the complete lack of ethics and complete lack of empathy.

"It's partly because the refugees have been thoroughly de-humanised in the way they've been dismissed, but also because they are not recognisable as human beings. They are nameless, faceless, they have no identity. They are simply a code number."

His attraction to the Labor Party, he says, was "partly a factor of my age". "I'm just old enough to remember the Depression of the 1930s and its horrors". In *A Thinking Reed*, he writes, "Even as a child, from my experience of seeing the squalor of Dudley Flats during the Great Depression, I started asking: 'Why are people living like this? Why are some people so poor and others (like us) not so poor? How can it be fixed?' Perhaps this ignited my preference for the politics of redistribution."

Now in his 85th year, with what he describes as "The Enlightenment Project" under threat, he is concerned about the rise of fundamentalism across the world, and that self-interest is increasingly placed before the common good.

He is also saddened, he says, "by the fact that the information revolution, instead of striving to encourage people towards the universal, has in fact emphasised the role of the personal and the immediate". "And you can see where fake news is important, because if you want to find something that says the earth is flat or vaccination is dangerous, you can find plenty of stuff, and say, 'There you are, there's my evidence'. I find that an absolute tragedy, a very limited view of the human capacity."

Education, he says, must be life-long, encourage creativity and teach us to tackle complexity. "This is something I write about in *The Shock of Recognition*. The fact is that now there is a kind of cultural attention on the simple. For example, much of the music people are exposed to now is overwhelmingly popular but it is extremely simple… But unless you start to develop a grasp of the complex, you're going to be permanently stunted."

The power of uniting Mary and Martha

Spanish mystic St Teresa of Avila is "one of the most remarkable women in the history of Christianity", according to world-renowned author of books on Christian mysticism, Emeritus Professor Bernard McGinn. He visited Melbourne, Australia, in 2015 as part of the celebrations to mark her 500th Anniversary, and spoke to Roland Ashby. The interview appeared in the September 2015 edition of *TMA*.

How did St Teresa, a "slacker" and "mediocre" nun in her early years, become the first woman to be made a Doctor of the Church (by Pope Paul VI in 1970)?

The answer, Professor McGinn told *TMA*, lies in the fact that Teresa became "a true contemplative-in-action. At the heart of her legacy is a deepening love of God and neighbour you attain through inner prayer and combining action with a sense of the presence of God."

"She taught us that the contemplative, or mystical, life is a part of the vocation of every Christian, whereas many people think of the mystical as something strange, totally out of the ordinary. However, the mystical is an essential element of faith which concerns the process of deepening the consciousness of God's presence in our lives and seeing its transforming effects."

Her devotion to inner prayer transformed Teresa, Professor McGinn says, from a "slacker, or 'mediocre religious' – as she described herself – into a shrewd operator", who, with the Inquisition looking over her shoulder, set up a reformed Carmelite Order, established 17 convents, and wrote her autobiography, the *Life*, and her mystical masterpiece, *The Interior Castle*.

Under her reforms, the sisters were required to spend at least two hours each day in silent, interior prayer, in addition to the daily corporate and liturgical prayers of the convent.

In the *Life*, she famously compared interior prayer and the soul's growing union with God to four stages of watering a garden. Professor McGinn explains: "It's a beautiful image of how we start from having to make our own effort to gradually being taken over by God's effort.

"The first stage… she likens to the labour of drawing water from a well. We have to get the water and water the garden ourselves.

"Supernatural, passive prayer begins with the second stage, which is like watering with a windlass. She calls this 'the prayer of quiet' because the faculties of the soul (memory, intellect and will) begin to be quieted as the will is being gradually united to God.

"The third stage is like water coming from a stream but, as in irrigation, we are still involved in directing it.

"However by the time we get to the fourth stage, it's raining. We're not doing it. It's God's gift. The rain is pouring down and we just have to stand and watch."

In her later work, *The Interior Castle*, Teresa describes the journey towards God as moving through seven rooms, or mansions, of a castle, with the seventh room, the centre of the castle, representing the centre of the soul where God resides. Professor McGinn: "God lives and glows within the centre of the soul, because this is the part of the soul which has been created in the image and likeness of God.

"This is the highest level of union where a spiritual marriage takes place between God and the soul. One of the effects of this is the perfect uniting of Mary and Martha. Teresa writes: 'Believe me, Martha and Mary must join together in order to show hospitality to the Lord and have him always present and not host him badly by failing to give him something to eat. How would Mary, always seated at his feet, provide him with food if her sister did not help her?'

"What is fundamental to recognise is that for Teresa, action and contemplation are not opposed modes of life, but are interdependent and united…"

How does Professor McGinn respond to theologian Noel O'Donoghue's comment that Teresa's union with God at the centre of the soul is "A kind of inebriation… The soul discovers that it is somehow deeply in love with God"?

"There is very much a sense of a deeper love of God throughout *The Interior Castle*," he says. "The language of inebriation is one of the most ancient languages in Christian mysticism, and part of it draws its inspiration from the Song of Songs, on which Teresa also wrote a commentary. Most of the mystics,

Teresa included, would emphasise that God is love, but this understanding also includes a new form of knowing God which is not knowing God in any discursive way that could be put into ordinary categories. It's a personal, intuitive knowing, a new kind of inner conviction that does not enable one to say more about God, but which has a deeper sense of knowing God as the Reality in one's life."

How important does he believe it is for us to model our own prayer lives on the seven stages outlined in *The Interior Castle*? "Teresa often says that the mansions she sketches are not the only path. God brings people by numerous paths and she is only describing her own.

"What was important to her was that prayer should be deeply centred on Christ and his passion and humanity. Even though God will sometimes give us a state of rapture, or ecstasy, where we're united to Christ but no longer conscious of him, we're still connected with him. She believed we should never give up the humanity of Christ, even though we can be drawn by divine grace into a state of absorption where we're no longer thinking about Christ's humanity."

He says that Teresa believed the ultimate test of our growth towards God is our growth in love for others – whether friends or enemies – as well as for the Cross.

"As she writes at the conclusion of *The Interior Castle*: 'In sum, my sisters… we should not build castles in the air. The Lord does not look so much at the greatness of our works as at the love with which they are done. And if we can do what we can, his Majesty will enable us each day to do more and more…'".

Neglect of Spirit impoverishes the faith

The Spirit is essential to our understanding of faith says renowned New Testament Scholar the Revd Canon Professor Dorothy Lee, who was appointed as the first Research Professor at Trinity College Theological School, Melbourne, Australia, in 2017. She spoke to Roland Ashby when she was Dean of the School for the June 2012 edition of *TMA*.

The Church needs to recover "the true experience of Spirit as the central priority in its life if it is to be true to itself, its Lord and its vocation," the late Benedictine monk John Main wrote in *Monastery without Walls*.

A new book, *Hallowed in Truth and Love*, by the Dean of Trinity College Theological School, the Revd Dr Dorothy Lee, explores this central place of Spirit for Christians, as seen in the Johannine Literature – the Gospel and Letters of St John, and the Book of Revelation.

Dr Lee told *TMA* that a unique aspect of John's Gospel is the use of the term *Paraclete*. "It is not found anywhere else in the New Testament except in 1 John, where it refers to Jesus himself. It is the term used to convey a profound sense of the personal presence of Jesus with the Church, when Jesus is with the Father. It is the answer to the experience of Jesus' absence – yes, he will come again, but he is already here in the form of the Paraclete, the Spirit, and to have the Spirit is to have the risen Christ still with the community."

The Spirit or Paraclete is not identical to Jesus, but mediator of his presence, she explains.

This notion of the Paraclete, she believes, "is absolutely essential for the life of the Church," something which the Western Church has not properly grasped. "I think it's been a bit of a problem in the Western Church that our theology hasn't been sufficiently Trinitarian. I'm amazed at listening to some

Christians speak as if there was only Jesus, and that's a problem to me. It's not enough to say we have Jesus, therefore we have everything. We don't. We have Father, Son and Holy Spirit."

It is the Spirit, she says, "which draws us into the love the Father has for the Son, and the Son has for the Father.

"I think the Eastern Church has understood this more completely, with its much stronger sense of God as Trinity. It has a much greater sense of Spirit in its theology, and a sense of constant presence of the Spirit – not just a sense of constant presence with us, but also in the whole creation."

This sense of the Spirit embodied in the physical, seen most perfectly in the Incarnation of Jesus, is key to understanding the spirituality of John's Gospel, Dr Lee says. "I think the centre of the Gospel is the Word became flesh and dwells among us (1:14). John sees the world as being created by the Word, who is the Son, what we later come to call the Second Person of the Trinity. But there's an implied gulf between us, and that we've somehow lost our identity as children of God, even though that's how we were created. The Incarnation is precisely what bridges the gulf between us and God.

"It's not just a gulf between us and God in terms of sin, alienation and death, but also it's a gulf because of our different natures. We are created beings, God is uncreated. We are temporal, God is eternal. The gulf is immeasurably complicated and made potentially tragic by our alienation from our Creator. So that when he comes among us, to paraphrase John, we fail to recognise him."

John's Gospel, she writes in *Hallowed in Truth and Love*, "has the capacity to reverberate into the present of any reader." She says that for her, this has largely been through symbol, something the Gospel is rich in. "Not symbol seen as a sort of spoonful of sugar that makes the medicine go down, but symbol as somehow substantial, as having content.

"This has deeply affected my understanding of liturgy and the sacraments, which have come to mean a lot more to me. Take, for example, John's emphasis on bread – Jesus himself is presented as the bread of life, and in John 6, we're called to eat the flesh and drink the blood of the Son of Man.

"To understand the Eucharist in this way has had a wonderfully transforming effect on me. Like all Johannine symbols it actually conveys what it points to. When I'm teaching I say 'it's not a sign pointing to Ballarat; it's both the sign pointing there and the bus that takes you there'.

"So I've had a profound sense in the Eucharist of the presence of Christ from understanding Jesus as the bread of life on whom we feast in order to have life.

"I think the sense of abiding has significantly affected my own sense of spirituality and of an ongoing relationship that's dependent, not primarily on me at all, but on the one who is divine. At the end of the day it's the vine that counts, and important for me to remain connected to the vine."

She prefers the word 'abide', she says, particularly when it is used in the sense of "Abide in me and I in you" (John 15:4), to 'remain', which is used by many translations, because "it suggests one's abode, which is one's home. It is the language of homecoming; it's where you are most at home, and the Father is most at home with the Son and the Son with the Father through His Spirit, and we are most at home with God, who has made his abode with us."

There are many symbols you can meditate on in the Gospel, she says, in the *lectio divina* style of slowly reading and re-reading the text, and 'chewing the cud'. "For example, you can read about the Samaritan woman (John 4:1-42) and identify with her experience. But you can also meditate on the symbol of water, and in what way you have that same spiritual thirst that she has, that underlies all her relationships and her messed up life. It may prompt some challenging questions: 'Where is my thirst for life? Where is my deepest thirst?'"

I comment that Jesus has some deeply moving and life-transforming encounters with women, so how does she respond as a woman to the Gospel?

"As a woman I think one of the great things about the Gospel is that it has such powerful women characters. The Samaritan woman is so feisty, and even cheeky, and yet comes to such a deep understanding.

"It's great to meet real women in the Gospel, who sometimes really struggle with their faith. Mary Magdalene, for example, even though she loves Jesus, fails to understand and can't read the signs.

"At the same time it's marvellous to be a woman to read, in this Gospel, that the one who says, 'You are the Christ' is a woman: it's Martha, not Peter."

Standing in a place where we can say 'thank you, God' for all that life holds

Prolific UK author of books on Christian spirituality, Esther de Waal, spoke to Roland Ashby about her book *Living on the Border – Reflections on the Experience of Threshold*, partly inspired by her return, in her later years, to the place of her birth – the border country between England and Wales. The interview appeared in the June 2013 edition of *TMA*.

With the approach of old age, thoughts naturally turn to the border or threshold between life and death – one of the themes explored by Esther de Waal in *Living on the Border*, which was originally published in 2001 but has been recently republished.

While Esther de Waal told *TMA* she was certainly apprehensive about dying – particularly as Alzheimer's runs in her family, and she fears that "half-living, half-dying state" – she writes in the Afterword to *Living on the Border* that "One of the pleasures of this stage of life's journey is the way in which all the threads of the tapestry begin to converge. Now, as I look back, past and present begin to merge and bring a new wholeness, a unity."

It has been a time of homecoming – returning to Herefordshire, on the border between England and Wales – where she grew up, providing inspiration for the book and its title. When she moved back after living in several cities, she says she was struck by "the simple reality of the land," and quotes H.J. Massingham: "Understanding a landscape is like getting to know a person. It's slow and needs time to draw out the personality."

Understanding the land for her has also been partly, she says, about appreciating how the Celts related to the land and understood time and the seasons. "The Celts marked the passing of time and seasons with great reverence and awareness. If you are aware of seasonal time, as they were, then you don't take for granted the generosity of a God who knows about creation and re-creation and the pattern of sowing, harrowing and harvesting."

She believes that Celts and Indigenous Australians "share in common a sense of relatedness to the land, and never of ownership, and the way in which they feel their connectedness to rocks, trees and above all, rivers, means that they have a sense of belonging, which is so often overlaid in a modern urban culture."

She was "hugely moved", she says, when she attended an event at the Uniting Church's Stillpoint Centre in Adelaide, which began with this acknowledgement of Indigenous Australians: "We believe that from ancient times God has sustained the life, spirit and promise of this land through these Aboriginal people."

But the most profound threshold or border in life, she believes, is that between the inner and outer, "between going deeper into the interior self and emerging to meet the world beyond the self without protective defences, as friend not as foe", she writes in *Living on the Border*.

She says an important reference for this inner journey has been the Rule of St Benedict, the famous sixth century guide for Benedictine monks. "It is ultimately a guide to homecoming to our life in Christ. It is about continual transformation or transfiguration into the likeness of Christ. And that, after all, is the ultimate purpose, I would hope, of any Christian discipleship."

A great metaphor for the inner meeting the outer, she says, is the porter at the gates of the monastery, who receives guests to the monastery and is a bridge to the outside world, and through whom there is a "conversation between the holy and the everyday".

"You picture him with one foot firmly anchored in the cloister, the enclosure, which means the pattern and rhythm of the day, and above all, a centrality of Opus Dei, saying the daily office.

"But the other foot is firmly planted on the other side of the doorway, in the world outside the monastery, and it is the holding of the two together that allows him to say 'Deo gratias. Thank God you have come' to whoever may come, seeing the Christ in them.

"And if I can, I sometimes like to extend the 'whoever may come' to welcoming the circumstances, the events, the next chapter, if you like, of one's life, which may appear at any time, not least unexpectedly, not of one's choosing.

"Only from the strength of the interior contemplative centre of prayer can one have the strength to say 'Deo Gratias' to the unwelcome events or circumstances of life."

Never forget common good, biblical ethics warn

George Browning, the retired Anglican Bishop of Canberra and Goulburn, Australia, believes the West's political system is failing to address our fundamental challenges. In his new book, *Sabbath and the Common Good – Prospects for a New Humanity*, he argues that recovering a 'Sabbath ethic' is the answer. He spoke to Roland Ashby for the June 2016 edition of *TMA*.

George Browning believes the crisis of the world today can be summed up as a "battle between self-interest and the thriving of common good", and in Western culture, he adds, "self-interest seems to be prevailing".

A fundamental problem for our culture and political system, he says, quoting theologian Lesslie Newbigin, is that economics is "no longer part of ethics [and] is not concerned with the purpose of human life".

"My fear is that politics is increasingly failing to play its proper role of regulating the market. The market is not *immoral*, it is *amoral*. The market is there to make profit, and the banking industry is there fundamentally for its shareholders, not its customers.

"A monetary value is placed on everything, and there is a tendency for us not to want to contribute to the common good. Politicians obviously feel that the vast majority of Australians want to pay less tax. Interestingly, though, significant people like Bernie Fraser are saying that's wrong; the population at large would be prepared to contribute to the common good if the narrative is explained to them properly, and common good means the well-being of the whole community, and all of life, including the whole natural environment."

The common good, he believes, is about shared blessing, inclusive of all creation, and not just blessing for oneself. He quotes Bible scholar Walter Brueggemann: "Persons living in a system of anxiety and fear – and consequently of greed – have no time or energy for the common good."

Bishop Browning says one of the great worries about the 21st century is whether "the inextricable growth in inequity is going to be allowed to go unchecked, because if it does, then I believe it's inevitable there'll be a massive reaction, both within human societies, and also in relation to the environment.

"Just one per cent of the world's population controls 90 per cent of the world's assets. As we have seen with the Panama Papers exposé, too many of these super-rich people are seeking to hide these assets and avoid contributing to the common good.

"This is a deplorable and frightening situation which is made worse by the fact that politics today is driven by wealth. Our democracy is in decline because those who have wealth employ lobbyists who have more influence on decision-making than the rest of us who vote every three years. Parliament is very much the home of the lobbyists."

He is particularly alarmed, he says, at how these vested interests have been able to exercise considerable influence over the shaping of environmental policy and action, even though the vast majority of climate scientists have been sounding the alarm for many years. "So, for example, one of the things that we need to do is to make certain that no more coal mines are opened and that we transition as quickly as we possibly can to a carbon-neutral world."

He believes that the two fundamental problems that undergird the environmental crisis are over-consumption and overpopulation. "The world cannot continue to consume at the level it is consuming. We cannot continue to consume more than the generation before us. Statistically, I think I consume twice as much as my grandfather.

"A moral challenge for us in the West is that we can't expect people in the developing world not to want to increase their consumption. It isn't our right to say they shouldn't. But we have to find a way to limit consumption because the world's resources are being consumed at a rate of about 140 to 150 per cent per annum. A debt to the future is being expanded every year; it simply cannot continue."

Population, too, he believes, has to be curbed. "The world cannot sustainably support a never-ending growth in population. In the West we think that economic growth is the only thing that matters, but economic growth is not possible in Australia without population expansion. Over the long term it is not sustainable. There has to be a disconnect between population expansion and economic activity."

As a former convener of the Anglican Communion's Environment Network he is passionate about the environment, and since childhood has felt a strong affinity with the natural world – having been brought up on a dairy farm in England and then later coming to Australia at the age of 18 to work as a jackeroo. He has a vivid memory, too, of consciously experiencing the transcendent through nature for the first time. "I was about 10 years old and had just started to help on the dairy farm. One morning, at about 5am, I was bringing out the cows and I had this overwhelming sense of Jacob's Ladder, and God somehow reaching down through the clouds. I have been greatly blessed and nurtured with this sense of the transcendent over the years."

It is a sense of the divine presence, he believes, that lies at the heart of humanity's salvation and the survival of the planet. "One of the underlying themes of *Sabbath and the Common Good* is the need for humanity to become aware of and experience what the Jews call *Shekinah*, the indwelling presence of God. This presence is in all relationships – with one another and all creation – and through this awareness we come to know that we all belong together. We are all the children of God. The Bible is quite clear that redemption relates to the whole created order, it doesn't relate simply to humanity.

"Because God is present, we need to behave as if God is present. This is why the Jews developed a theology of Sabbath – in response to the *Shekinah*."

The Sabbath ethic, he says, is not so much about the 'seventh' day of creation, but about the previous 'six', how humans treat the land and one another. "It has to do with release from slavery and debt as in the idea of Jubilee. Debt is seen as an abuse of power.

"An important commandment implicit to this ethic is 'You shall not covet', which is about allowing space for the other. When you're 'in somebody's face', you deny that person space. Covetousness is denying somebody else's space.

"In the life of Jesus we see the one who creates space for us all, the one who forgives debt; the one, most specifically on the cross, who decrees that those who are crushed who find no space for themselves, are the ones above all who are to be set free."

In *Sabbath and the Common Good* he writes: "Jesus' sayings indicate he was arguing for a jubilee way of life. The beatitudes are a mandate for a life of jubilee, lived and expressed within a context where disempowerment is most pressing... Christ's mission to and with the whole world is for its harmony and wholeness, its reimagining and redeeming, its blessing and hallowing. This is a vision of Sabbath fulfilled."

Christ's selfless love – shown supremely in his *Kenosis*, or self-emptying, on the cross – is the very nature of God. Our vocation as followers of Christ, he argues, must therefore be characterised by sacrificial selfless love.

"We cannot be true to that vocation unless we rediscover holiness as engagement. Blessed are not the ones who sit on their backsides at home sheltered by their own possessions, but blessed are those who are engaging with the community at large. Blessed are those who are striving for the common good of humanity and the whole natural environment."

....

Sabbath and the Common Good – Prospects for a New Humanity *is published by Echo Books.*

Sharing a history with God

The Revd Dr Graham Cole is Dean of Trinity Evangelical Divinity School, Illinois, USA and Professor of Biblical and Systematic Theology. Here he talks to Roland Ashby about C.S. Lewis' idea of the 'lived-through proof' – the accumulation over time of personal stories of how God has been real. The interview appeared in the November 2001 edition of *TMA*, following his completion of nine years as Principal of Ridley College, Melbourne, Australia.

RA: How has God been real to you?

GC: My own experience has been a very real one. I think it illustrates to me the lived-through proof idea of C.S. Lewis, because my own conversion to Christ was a dramatic one, and an amazing turnaround in my life.

In my last year of high school, one of my school friends was converted. He was actually a very nasty piece of work, and the change in his life was undeniably for the good. He and some of his new Christian friends invited me along to their church because they had a special service. I went along and that night the preacher just spoke very simply about the cross, about the problem of our sin and the need for forgiveness and what it cost God to provide a way back to himself through Christ's death.

When I went home that night I just had an overwhelming sense that God hadn't turned his back on the world as I had thought, but I had turned my back on God. So I cried out to God that night, "Don't forsake me!". I can only say that I went to sleep with those words on my lips and when I woke up the next day I was a different person. By a different person I mean that I couldn't lie any more to people, I had to tell them the truth. And I had to go and tell lots of people the truth about things I had said to them, and there was a whole range of things I just could no longer do. So it was dramatic.

Over the last thirty or so years of Christian life I have found over and over again the truth of that psalmist, "I love the Lord because he answers my prayer" (Psalm 116:1).

In the early days as a Christian I loved reading all the books of arguments for the faith. They were extremely helpful to me in the early years of my following Christ because, amongst other things, I knew so little about the Christian faith and the content of the Bible and Christian history and so on. But now after thirty years, although those arguments are still very important and I teach them in class, they don't move me the way they once did because ultimately I have shared a history with God.

And with the postmodernist person, I find that's really what they are interested in. They are not so interested in the modernist-style argument – here's the evidence, this is what it leads to, it is more probable that Christ rose from the dead than he didn't and so what are you going to do about it? They are more interested in the relevance that you have found in Christ, and the only way to really address that with the postmodern people, I find, is to tell them your story.

So I find with postmodern people the biblical practice of giving your testimony, of saying "once I was blind but now I see," is the crucial practice. But you still meet the person shaped by modernity, the person who asks, where is the evidence? Where is the proof? For that sort of person you still need to talk about truth, not just relevance, because they rightly argue that you can make mistakes and be self-deceived about the relevance of something. I still find all those arguments very handy, and therefore I have really got two kinds of audience I find myself engaging with – people with whom I need to talk about the truth of the faith, and here's why, shaped by modernity; and those to whom I need to tell my story because they won't really even have an interest unless they see it makes a real difference to me.

RA: How does being a Christian make a difference in terms of how you cope with suffering and the problem of evil in the world? Before the interview you told me the events of 11 September had left you feeling flat and had affected you deeply. How as a Christian do you find consolation?

GC: I have found it in two cases – let me not be abstract about this. I am 52 and if I hadn't actually experienced the problem of evil at a personal level by the age of 52 then I must be a very unusual person. By that I mean that by age 52 if I haven't had my own personal cancer scare, had to bury parents, worry about kids, almost get killed on the road or whatever, I would be a pretty unusual person, and I am not. So I will tell a personal story and then relate it to this much, much bigger story about New York and the Pentagon.

In 1983-84 my wife and I went through a dreadful personal experience. And so I asked the question, where is God? Just like the psalmist – "How long O Lord?" – or the prophet – "O that you would rend the heavens and come down".

It's a biblical question. One of the great strengths of the Bible is, as Samuel Taylor Coleridge put it, it gives us a language for our joys and our sorrows, for every area of life, and the language it gives us in our puzzlement and our pain and our sorrow is the language of lament.

I found that language of lament very real, and it has questions like that: Where is God? – the sort of question being asked at the moment. I can say that I found God in two places. I found God in the stories of the Bible, supremely the story of the cross, that God knows pain and suffering and alienation on the inside.

But I also found God in the body of Christ, because when I asked the question "Where is the actual embrace of God in all this?" it was through people who came and prayed with us, who came to be with us to show concern or help in some way. When I re-read the Bible in the light of that, I came across something Paul said in 2 Corinthians 7. He said the God who comforts the downcast (because if you read that letter he was quite depressed at times) comforted us through the coming of Titus.

I have come to the view that we Christians are the body language of the invisible Christ, that's part of our responsibility. And so when I find that one of the people who perished in New York was the chaplain of the Fire Department, I know God's people are real and God has real skin on.

I think we have a gut feeling that if God created everything he is responsible, and I think that intuition is right. So I would argue that God is responsible for the problem of evil. But I think there is a distinction between being responsible and being culpable. God hasn't done the evil, but evil has been done in this good world and he is responsible that evil doesn't triumph and that good will come out of it.

The human journey is not yet over, and the journey of the universe, creation, is not yet over. But by the end of it all God will need to be seen as the responsible God who has actually done something about the eruption of evil in His good world. And again the story of Jesus is the great pledge that he is indeed on that job.

RA: In the course you teach on apologetics you draw a distinction between certitude and certainty and argue that some philosophers in rejecting God make a 'category mistake'.

GC: Yes, I think there's an important distinction between certainty and certitude, one which I work with very much. Certainty has to do with the logical force of any argument and why it's believable. Certitude has to do with our psychological sense of assurance that we are on the right track, we've made a real connection, this is really true.

There are some areas of human inquiry where the logical force of our arguments is not as strong as our actual sense of confidence that we have got it right.

A number of people who are sceptical about Christianity want to say that our certainty has to be exactly the same in force as our certitude, otherwise we are being irresponsible in claiming to believe what we believe is right.

But the folk who say that, I tend to find, come out of the science background. They confuse what we are claiming to be true with mathematical claims such as two plus two equals four, or the sort of stuff you can repeat in the laboratory, such as an acid added to an alkaline produces salt and water time and time again.

The Christian claim about Christ having been raised from the dead is more like the claim that our best friend is really trustworthy, or my wife or my husband is really faithful to me.

When you present an argument to back that up, the force of the argument will never be a knockdown proof like acid plus an alkaline equals salt plus water, or two plus two equals four, and there is a gap, if you like, between the certainty we can present in an argument, its logical force, and certitude, our confidence.

I think one reason why that happens, that the certitude can legitimately exceed our certainty, the force of our arguments, is that as a Christian, the longer you actually live with God as a real person you engage with in your prayer and your life, you have access to a history that the person on the outside you are presenting your arguments to doesn't have.

The philosophers would say you have an 'internalist' account you can give of what you believe. I love what the psalmist says: "I love the Lord because he answered my prayer."

I think that C.S. Lewis, in his idea of the lived-through proof, meant that as you live with God over time you develop a fund of personal stories of how God has been real to you. This is really what makes a certitude that goes beyond just arguments for the Resurrection.

RA: Francis Schaeffer said that Christianity isn't just about truth but about love, and love is the final apologetic.

GC: I have been very impressed with the way Schaeffer, the American evangelist and apologist who was largely based in Switzerland and had a worldwide ministry, sought to address this question.

He thought, I think rightly, that it is not enough to simply say Christianity is true, and it is not enough to simply give your reasons for thinking it is true. You actually have to live as though it is true, as though God really is love, that Christ really did teach us to love our neighbours as ourselves.

And that means that our claims about God's character and Christ need to be embodied in community. So in Switzerland he established his L'Abri community – 'L'Abri' means shelter – in which hospitality was extended to all, whether they were 'druggies' or unmarried pregnant mothers-to-be or whatever, and he practised there what he called "the beauty of relationships".

I think in our postmodern world where talk is cheap, and where many have been influenced by the postmodern way of thinking, what will impress them will be the beauty of our relationships, and that's a challenge to the Church.

How have we loved? In the end it's all that matters

When he invited two men with disabilities to share his life, it transformed former naval officer Jean Vanier, as he explains to his long-time disciple Maggie Fergusson. The interview appeared in the April 2018 edition of TMA.

The Scots have a word for those places where the veil between heaven and earth seems almost transparent. They call them "thin" places; and there can be few "thinner" places than the village of Trosly-Breuil, less than 40 miles north of Paris, on the edge of the forest of Compiègne.

Many readers will be familiar with the story. In 1964, a tall, handsome, ex-naval officer, Jean Vanier, was invited to Trosly to visit an asylum for men with mental disabilities. "It was a horrific place," he says, "full of screaming and violence; and yet it filled me with a sense of wonderment. I sensed in these men a great cry – 'Do you love me?', 'Will you come back?'" He visited other asylums, equally dismal, and then decided to act.

"What I love about the Good Samaritan," Vanier says, "is that he didn't waste time weighing up the pros and cons, he just did something." He himself was similarly bold. Having bought a tumbledown cottage in Trosly, he invited two men with disabilities – Raphaël Simi and Philippe Seux – to leave their asylum and live with him. He called their home L'Arche, "the ark".

"There was no huge idea," he says, "no intention to change the world." He simply wanted to ease the suffering of two men. But, as he shared his life with Raphaël and Philippe, he gradually discovered that he was being transformed by them. "God has chosen the weak and the foolish," he says, rephrasing St

Paul, "to confound those caught up in their heads." Raphaël and Philippe were enabling him to live from his heart, to escape "the tyranny of normality", to laugh like a child. They were, he says, "teachers of tenderness". Others came to join him, the community grew.

Today there are 143 L'Arche communities in 35 countries, from Zimbabwe to Palestine, Uganda to the UK. In each one, "normal" people live as assistants to people with disabilities. While Vanier is a devout Catholic, L'Arche welcomes people of all religions and none: "My feet are rooted in my faith, but my arms are wide open," Vanier says. "What is important is not necessarily a belief in God, but a capacity to love people as they are. You can not believe in God, but still believe in relationship."

Vanier still lives in Trosly. Now 88, he is white-haired and slightly stooped, but his mind is crystal clear. "People who are old," he has written, "and offer themselves to God, can become lightning conductors of grace." He did not write this as a description of himself, but it is a good one. To visit him in his little sitting room is to feel oneself in the presence of almost palpable holiness. Around him on the floor are books and correspondence; to his left, on a pin board, pictures of men and women who have inspired him: Aung San Suu Kyi, Etty Hillesum, Sophie Scholl, Gandhi.

There is no computer, no iPad, no mobile. "We've become experts in communication," Vanier says, "but we're not so good at presence." Undistracted by technology, he gives every visitor his full, steady attention, and you come away from seeing him with an uncanny feeling that he knows you better than you know yourself. Meetings needn't be long. Sometimes it takes just 10 minutes' conversation to shift some logjam of confusion or sadness.

Vanier has been listening to people's difficulties for 53 years now. Aren't there times, I wonder, when he feels he simply cannot absorb any more pain? "I don't think I do absorb pain," he says. "If you absorb pain too much you can lose something of your identity. But often when I meet people it's a healing experience for me. I'm not a healer or a curer; all I can be is a good listener. And that seems to be the healing part for people – that somebody appreciates them.

"Most people are caught up in guilt – there's a whole element of anger against self, broken self-image, the guilt of existence. So in listening to people you're going through a barrier of self-disgust. My life in L'Arche has taught me that everybody is beautiful. Everybody. So to love people is to reveal to them that they are more beautiful than they dare believe." Is anybody beyond this love? "People say, 'How can we love terrorists?' But most terrorists have been deeply wounded, or humiliated, living in lands where people reject their cultures. We must pray for them."

I first came to Trosly as an assistant more than 20 years ago, and I have visited once or twice a year since then. Recently I fulfilled a long-held wish to join a week-long retreat on the Gospel of St John, led in English by Vanier. There were 40 of us, from all over the English-speaking world, and on the first evening, tired and tetchy from London, I found myself making harsh, involuntary judgements about my fellow retreatants. This man seemed pleased with himself; that woman talked too much. Then, as the week unfolded – two talks a day from Vanier, plenty of rest, hours of silence – I began to see them in a new light.

"Most men live lives of quiet desperation," Henry Thoreau wrote. But I wonder whether it's truer to say that most men, most people, live lives of quiet heroism. Almost everyone on the retreat – from the woman abused as a child, to the man bringing up twin teenage boys with Down's syndrome and ADHD – told a story of extraordinary courage. And all of us felt, as the week went on, a great letting-down of barriers and lightening of the spirit. How, I asked Vanier, could we hang on to this back in the "real" world?

"We all have a need, very fundamental, to prove that we are someone. But gradually we have to let the ego descend and the spirit rise up. It's a long road. Buddha says that the man who conquers one million men in battle is less of a conqueror than the man who conquers his ego. And we need, through prayer, to be attentive to the 'little voice' that Newman speaks about – the voice with which God speaks to every human heart. Can we hear the voice, or are we too busy – addicted to doing things? We need to be disciplined."

Vanier grew up with an extraordinary model of discipline. His father, Georges Vanier, who was Governor General of Canada – and whom Lord Mountbatten described as "the greatest Canadian of his time" – set aside half an hour each day for silent prayer, and attended daily Mass. And Jean himself, for all his gentleness and good humour, is formidably tidy with his time. In all the years I've known him, he's never once been late for a meeting. During the retreat, he arrived a little early for each talk, and at the end of every day, after darkness had fallen, he slipped into the small candlelit chapel next to his house to end his day in front of the Blessed Sacrament.

But prayer is best twinned with action. As we settled into our retreat, Jean invited us gently to reflect on three questions: Where are the poor in my life? Who are the poor to me? And how am I a consoler for the weak and the suffering? Each one of us, he urged, can make a difference – "even if only in the way we look at people. When you pass someone begging in the street, for example, it's not a question of 'Do you give him euros?' so much as 'Do you really look at him as a human being?' When you begin to let people who are 'no good' into your life, you are transformed."

By opening ourselves to others' pain, Jean suggested, we would be drawn into the mystery that suffering and joy are symbiotic. "Visitors are often surprised at the joy they sense in L'Arche," he has written. "It surprises me too because I know how much suffering some people in our communities are carrying. I wonder then if all joy doesn't somehow spring from suffering and sacrifice."

None of us on the retreat was conventionally poor. But there are regular retreats in Trosly for which Jean welcomes 40-odd homeless people from Paris, and – most moving of all, according to Rick Hatem, one of the assistants – retreats for gay couples. I wonder whether Jean's thinking about homosexuality has altered over the years. Not on laws, he answers, but on individuals. "I've listened to people, deeply wonderful people, and to hear them talking of their pain: rejected by the family, laughed at at school! I went into a prison recently where there were a lot of tough guys – you can imagine – and then one guy whom you saw immediately was fragile and closer to the feminine. And you just know what he has suffered… So what we can do is to listen to people, and hear what they've lived, and then begin to understand. And not to judge. Never judge."

Jean will turn 90 next year. He reckons he's "OK 'til I'm 94/95". Though the day must come when he can no longer visit prisons or give retreats, he is not afraid of it: "I know that every loss brings a gain." But what about old people who do not share his equanimity? During the retreat, the BBC carried a news item about a man with motor neurone disease, Noel Conway, challenging the UK ban on assisted dying. What would Jean say to people in great pain who want help in ending their lives? "I don't know what I'd say. But perhaps somewhere they haven't really been helped. All I know is that in my experience in L'Arche – and I can only talk from experience – people who are terribly depressed and in great pain are transformed when they know they are really loved."

And what about people – like my mother, who died in April – who grow frightened towards the end? What happens to us when we die? Jean is wonderfully clear. "When you die, you fall asleep. And you wake up, and there's a very gentle peace. You feel well. And then you discover the face of God coming through that 'wellness'. Of course, we are outside time, so it's not sequential. Seeing Jesus' face, we suddenly have a feeling of having hurt him – we realise we could have done much better, we've done wrong. We are not being judged, we judge ourselves. But then comes the realisation that we are loved just as we are, in our darkness. So there's a meeting with God, who loves us in our poverty – and this we can hardly believe. That meeting brings an immense desire to be closer. That desire becomes a place of desire – I think of Purgatory as 'the place of desire' – and it's painful. When you have desire and not the object of desire, it's very painful. But then the desire augments, and consequently the pain augments, until there is a moment of explosion, and then we're in communion with God."

And hell?

"I can't speak about hell, but wasn't it John Paul II who said that, even if hell exists, it may be empty?"

The retreat flashed by. Over the final lunch, we chatted about the wisdom and insights we hoped to carry home. Looking across the room at Jean, listening and laughing, I thought of something he had said earlier in the week: "When we die, it's not a question of what we've done, but of how we've loved."

Maggie Fergusson is the literary director of the Royal Society of Literature. This is a slightly edited version of an article which first appeared, with the heading 'Surprised by Joy', in the 28 October 2017 edition of The Tablet: The International Catholic News Weekly. *See http://www.thetablet.co.uk It is reproduced with the permission of the publisher.*

Photo credit: Kit Haselden

Justin Welby reflects on prayer and suffering

During a very busy one-day visit to Melbourne, Australia, in August 2014, Archbishop of Canterbury Justin Welby managed to find a brief time to talk to Roland Ashby about his understanding of prayer and contemplation, and how suffering – including the death of his daughter – can be reconciled with faith. The interview appeared in the September 2014 edition of *TMA*.

RA: When you became Archbishop of Canterbury you said your first priority was the renewal of prayer and the religious life. This obviously reflects the high priority you have given to prayer and spirituality in your own life. You attended a famous charismatic Church – Holy Trinity Brompton; you are a Benedictine Oblate; and you have also talked about the influence of Ignatian spirituality on your own development. Could you please explain how each of these elements has shaped your prayer life and your understanding of prayer?

JW: The key thing for me, as I've grown as a Christian, has been in understanding that no particular style or tradition has a monopoly on everything there is about prayer; and through very good spiritual direction – being well directed from time to time and challenged – understanding the importance of being able to draw on the wealth of the breadth of Christian spirituality.

How has that affected my prayer life? By learning to recognise, for instance, the importance of silence, as well as passionate intercessory prayer; by learning to recognise the place of the charismatic elements of spirituality, of the spiritual gifts in particular, and in private prayer the use of speaking in tongues.

That one is praying in ways that are not always comfortable is very important in order to ensure that we do not simply become routine in our prayers but are engaging with the person of God rather than with our own habits.

RA: Do you meditate on scripture using the Benedictine method of Lectio Divina?

JW: Yes I do – very much so: just chewing over and over a passage, looking at a word, staying with it for long periods of time.

RA: And the Ignatian way, imaginatively placing yourself in a scene?

JW: Yes, but if I'm being honest, I'm slightly less disciplined about doing that but I find, particularly when I come to a place where I'm stuck with a passage or it seems stale… to use that Ignatian tradition of putting yourself in the [passage or story as one of the protagonists or as an observer] is hugely important.

RA: The 20th century mystic Thomas Merton said that "contemplation is a sudden gift of awareness, an awakening to the Real within all that is real. A vivid awareness of Infinite Being at the roots of our own limited being. An awareness of our contingent reality as received, as a present from God, as free gift of love". What do you understand contemplation to be, and what is your own experience of contemplation?

JW: My understanding is that contemplation is allowing the spirit of God to draw one into the presence of God with no intention except the enjoyment of that presence, with enjoying the presence of God as an end in itself. And it is a gift. It's something that sometimes – I hate to use the word 'works' – is there and sometimes it's not. Sometimes it's a huge struggle; sometimes somehow one finds oneself there.

RA: So clearly a sense of it as gift?

JW: There is a huge sense of it as gift, but then all prayer is gift. There is no prayer that is not gift, because everything is Grace. The moment we think we're doing some of it ourselves, even a scrap of it, and are not utterly dependent on the Grace of God, it's mere words, it's mere talking to the ceiling.

RA: You have obviously made the renewal of prayer your first priority rather than evangelism because you have said that conversion is the fruit of evangelism and witness but "utterly the work of the Holy Spirit." Would you expand on that please?

JW: Evangelism arises out of the overflow of our own experience and knowledge of the love of Christ. When we know and experience that we have been loved and saved and rescued and are loved, we seek to share that because it is so special. It's not something like brushing our teeth every day, it's something that is an overflow. For that overflow to happen there's got to be an inflow, and the inflow is in prayer.

RA: For many people suffering is the great stumbling block to faith, particularly the suffering and death of children. You had a young daughter who died in a car accident. How have you reconciled this with your faith?

JW: I've reconciled it, if I have, both badly and well. The bad bit is simply to say, 'Well it's a tough world and bad things happen and we have to learn to live with that.' Probably the better way of looking at it is saying, that through the incarnation, and above all through his death on the cross, we see the presence of Christ in the midst of the most extreme suffering and he himself taking on the suffering of the whole world.

There is a verse that spoke very deeply to my wife when our daughter died: Psalm 56: Verse 8, which in one translation is, *He stores up our tears in a bottle*. Nothing is wasted before God, even our suffering. It doesn't make it any easier to bear. There are some friends of ours at the moment whose son, who is in his 20s, is terribly ill. The agony they are going through is indescribable, and there are no painless answers to it, there is no quick fix; but God goes through it with us, and in the end evil is never greater than his capacity to overturn the most evil thing, such as our daughter's death or what is happening in Iraq now with ISIS, and somehow to be there in the midst of it and to bring light into the midst of it.

....

See more information on Lectio Divina and Ignatian spirituality at: www.melbourneanglican.org.au/faith/CallingMelbourne2Prayer/Pages/Prayer-resources.aspx and Benedictine Oblates see: www.osb.org/obl/intro.html

Photo credit: Jan Down

Church a place of 'grace and healing' despite abuse scandals

The Most Revd Kay Goldsworthy AO became Australia's first female archbishop when she was installed as Archbishop of Perth in Western Australia on 10 February 2018. The former Bishop of Gippsland, Victoria, spoke to Emma Halgren about her path to ordination, and the challenges facing the Church in the wake of the Royal Commission into Institutional Responses to Child Sexual Abuse. The interview appeared in the December 2017 edition of *TMA*.

The church's place in the community has changed and is continuing to change, and in the wake of sexual abuse scandals it must work anew at building trust, says Bishop Kay Goldsworthy. The church is in a "season of repentance" for the abuses of trust it has been part of.

"For many people the church is a place in which there is light and life and grace and healing and fullness, and the love of Christ is very real, but we also know that there has been a lot that has not been okay in any way at all, that has not been good," she said.

"And so, what shape we will be, I think none of us knows; what we are becoming, we don't know; but it is going to be looking different and the world around us is, day by day by day, I think, announcing how very different we need to be and from what we've been, in some ways."

As Archbishop of Perth she will succeed Roger Herft, who announced last December that he would retire early. Archbishop Herft had stood aside as Archbishop of Perth in October 2016 so that he could focus fully on the public hearing into the Diocese of Newcastle, in New South Wales – where he had been bishop from 1993 to 2005 – by the Royal Commission into Institutional Responses to Child Sexual Abuse.

Being elected Australia's first female archbishop is the latest in a series of firsts for Bishop Goldsworthy. She was among the country's first women priests, ordained in 1992, and in 2008 became Australia's first female bishop, when she was consecrated as an assistant bishop of Perth.

But she said she had always felt strongly that she was in the "company of others" — men and women who were supportive of women's ordination, and women who, like her, were taking up ordained ministry roles in the church.

"When it became clear to me that I thought that God was calling me to be a priest… I really felt that I was part of something that was quite challenging. There was a lot of heat around in the early 1980s over all of this [women's ordination], a lot of heat and a lot of concern and a lot of determination that many, many people believed that this was where God was calling the church.

"As an individual and as somebody young and just starting out in formation and training and wondering, the church feels like a pretty big thing in the face of all of that. However, I've always felt that I've been in the company of others."

Bishop Goldsworthy grew up in Melbourne, attending first Holy Trinity Kew and then, as a teenager, St Francis-in-the-Fields Mooroolbark, a parish she described as having been "very formative" in her life.

"At a particular age as a young teenager, my parish priest had a fantastic ministry for me and for other people of my age. It was a ministry which said, 'you're taken seriously, your questions are taken seriously, never think you have a question that's too big to bring to God, to the Bible, to faith. It may take some time to work out how you answer that or find an answer, but there's nothing that can't be brought'. That was a very freeing thing for me."

At home, her mother imparted a strong message about the power of prayer and of God's love. Her father had a chronic illness and for Bishop Goldsworthy as a young person, prayer was a way of responding to his illness and her concern for him.

"I don't really remember a time when the language of God and the language of Jesus wasn't part of our household," she said. "I grew up in a house where people spoke about God, where people talked about prayer. The overwhelming message in my household was that God loves you."

Bishop Goldsworthy received her theological training at Melbourne's Trinity College, where she was one of the last generation of residential theological students. "My experience as a member of a community of formation students, who were all in the midst of testing vocation and searching, was a very particular one because it meant praying with each other day by day and living in community in a very particular way, not a community set apart, but a community set in the midst of other students and the university. I studied at, as it was then, the United Faculty of Theology ecumenical community and that also has been part of the shaping and forming, having been taught by Anglicans and members of the Uniting Church and mostly Jesuits from the Catholic community. That was a stunning experience."

Bishop Goldsworthy has indicated that one of her priorities when she becomes Archbishop of Perth will be to look at what the diocese is doing to care for and support victims of family violence. She said that the church had an important role to play in addressing violence in the home, and that it was "terrifying" that in some cases, interpretations of biblical texts had been used by perpetrators to justify their actions.

"If you tell people they have a particular place and you preach that from your pulpit, it can be taken on board in ways that people never intend, but that land really dangerously, really dangerously. And, of course, what that means is that women are hearing particular messages about how they should be in family and community.

"Now what I know is that the church that I'm part of, and have been part of for all of my life, is a place where many people who have experienced abuse and violence have found hope and they have found welcome and they have found a place of new understandings of how it can be that God sees them and sees their place, and they have been able to heal and be set free in all sorts of ways that have just been wonderful. That's part of what I know about the church as well. It's good news."

Emma Halgren is Deputy Editor of TMA and a freelance writer and editor. She has worked for more than 15 years in communications in not-for-profit and church organisations in Sydney, Geneva and Melbourne. She has studied politics, journalism and theology.

Religion/spirituality split weakening Christianity

A major challenge for Christianity today is that a split has occurred between religion and spirituality, argues Kim Nataraja, author and international school co-ordinator for the World Community for Christian Meditation, based in the UK. She spoke to Roland Ashby for the April 2007 edition of *TMA*.

RA: You have said that Christianity, particularly in the West, needs to rediscover the spirituality experienced by the early church fathers, who were contemplatives.

KN: What people often forget is that Christianity is a religion based on the spiritual experience of one man, namely Jesus – and it is the spiritual experience of being totally at one with God. So that is the start. Jesus himself was a contemplative, he prayed in communion but he went out into the hills to pray by himself. So we see mirrored in Jesus the communal prayer and the individual prayer which are essential for relationship with God.

All the early church fathers and mothers saw the contemplative tradition as an essential linking back to this experience of Jesus. And all the theology, all the thinking they did about God was based on their deep prayer with the scriptures. The important link between the scriptures and prayer must not be underestimated. The Fathers of the second and third centuries, the Cappadocian Fathers and Clement and Origen – all of them received their knowledge of God through their intuitive knowledge of scripture. They felt that scripture was the meeting ground with Christ and so they would read, absorb and relate it to themselves and then that would lead to the really deep prayer of silence where they found Christ within.

And so one of the sayings of the early church was 'the theologian is one who prays and one who prays is a theologian.' Matthew 6:6 was an important Bible passage for them. Where it says 'when you pray go into your room, shut the door...' that was very much for the early church fathers and especially the desert fathers and mothers of the fourth century the key teaching and they saw the room as your own heart. They explained that shutting the door meant shutting your lips and eyes so that you go within, into the silence which is God. And they quote verses such as 'be still and know that I am God' and quote Elijah hearing God not in the wind, and all the noise, but in the still, small voice of calm. It is sometimes translated as the 'sheer sound of silence.'

So contemplation is very much part of Christianity. And for those who have never heard about it I would say it is the listening part of prayer. We are told to ask God for things, praise him, thank him, and intercede on behalf of others – but we don't actually listen to God. Christ is our friend – so how would you feel about a friend who always talks at you and never listens to you? I think that contemplative prayer which we sometimes call Christian meditation comes out of this listening.

RA: Christian meditation perhaps began with Lectio Divina, which is meditation on scripture and a deep engagement with scripture.

KN: Lectio Divina is very much a Benedictine discipline which goes back in fact to the tradition in the desert and the early church fathers. It was a way in the early centuries of listening to scripture being read out, because it was an oral culture and many were illiterate. Then they would try to repeat it silently to themselves, which they then called meditation – not in a way that we do, an analytical sort of perception of it – but just a gentle repeating, and out of that something would resonate and become prayer and that would lead you into the silence. The whole process of Lectio Divina is a process of prayer starting from scripture, then relating to God, and then being silent with God, and being in his presence.

RA: Another form of Christian meditation uses a mantra. For many Christians the idea of a mantra can be off-putting because it's something they associate with eastern mysticism or the New Age.

KN: Yes, but with everything in life you've got to set it in context. When John Main, the Benedictine Monk who founded the World Community of Christian Meditation in the early 70s started talking about Christian meditation he did so because at the time all you heard about was Buddhist meditation, Transcendental meditation and Hindu Meditation, and he wanted to make it clear that Christianity also had a practice of meditation. That's why he called it Christian meditation rather than contemplative prayer.

His use of the word mantra is really the same. Everyone was saying 'What's your mantra?' What are you using? So he used a word which people at the time could relate to. But in our tradition of Christian meditation as rediscovered by John Main, the mantra is not just something repeated. It's a prayer. And that is the important essence. If you go back to the first few centuries there is a lot of emphasis in the Christian writing about using few words in prayer. Indeed, Jesus himself told us to use few words, and not to 'babble on like the heathens'. He also told us the story of the Pharisee and the publican, in which the only words the publican prays are 'Oh God, have mercy on me a sinner.' Jesus then said that that man is justified. It was the few words in prayer said with true longing, with depth of love, that Jesus said was the way to pray.

In Christian meditation the aim is to repeat the prayer word, the mantra, with this deep, longing love to be in the presence of God. And of course it has side benefits. If you really pay attention to your prayer word, your mantra, then it leads you in the silence because you can't think other thoughts. Your other thoughts disappear. And that is in fact an experience of leaving self behind which is what Jesus also asked us to do. If you focus on prayer you leave thoughts of self behind and you just stay in the present moment in the presence of Christ. That is the point of the mantra.

RA: John Main explained what was happening in meditation in beautiful Trinitarian terms.

KN: Very much indeed. In fact, he is completely in line with orthodox theology. What is happening in the time of meditation will vary for each person. But as John Main said, in Trinitarian terms what happens is that by repeating your prayer you enter the silence in the centre of your being where the Spirit of Christ dwells. And there you enter the stream of love which is the Holy Spirit between the Father and the Son. So the whole prayer is not *your* prayer – you join in the prayer of Christ with the Spirit. So it is beautifully Trinitarian.

RA: Meditation is a powerful form of healing. Could you say something about how meditation helps in our psychological healing?

KN: Yes. The condition we are in nowadays is that we are very focussed on our rational, logical self. That is good, and that is the way that we live in the world, that's the way we survive. But it can also lead to a tremendous fragmentation of our being, because we are a lot more than just our logical, rational being. We are the temple of the Holy Spirit. Unfortunately we've forgotten that we are spiritual beings and that we are children of God. Although it is said in scripture people just don't believe it of themselves any more. But I think the whole essence of my book *Dancing with your Shadow* is to say to people 'Come on, believe this, you are a beloved child of God.' That's the essence of your being.

I use the Jungian term 'Shadow' in the book to describe all the forgotten and rejected parts of ourselves which the ego has repressed. These tend to manifest when we project feelings or thoughts onto others, when we blame or judge others, when we search for our perceived unmet needs for love and security in wealth and possessions and addictions and possessiveness, or are driven by false images of ourselves.

In meditation there is an opportunity to encounter, and even embrace, this Shadow. It can be very painful, but it is very healing. But of course in this process of healing you need the help of the beautiful therapist – Christ – who dwells within. You cannot do it on your own.

RA: In your book you talk about a traumatic experience you had as a child. Has meditation been a source of healing for you?

KN: Very much. Meditation has enabled me to see the woundedness we all have not as any punishment of God but just an inevitable result of being alive. It has helped me to see that all of our woundedness is held and enveloped by God. So I am able to face life from this point of security of being loved – whatever life throws at me. And so this is really what I pray for – that all people may have this real feeling that they are beloved of God. And you find that in the silence and stillness of meditation – when the chattering mind has been silenced. Then we become aware of the Spirit within and we can hear the still, small voice.

....

For more information on Christian meditation see
www.christianmeditationaustralia.org

Looking death in the face without fear

Our culture is in denial about death, even though it is obsessed with it, according to Laurence Freeman, Benedictine Monk, Director of the World Community for Christian Meditation and author of *Jesus the teacher within*. He spoke to Roland Ashby for the May 2010 edition of *TMA*.

More than 160 million people died as a direct result of war in the 20th century, and many more who survived suffered from psychological trauma, Laurence Freeman says. "So perhaps our culture's denial of death is a natural result of the incredible increase in our capacity to kill people."

He adds that our obsession with death is also explained by the denial. "Our repression of the fear of death is reflected in our culture of violence and our very strange and sadistic enjoyment of violence as entertainment, and the increasingly graphic representation of it on TV, in film, and even more disturbingly, in the video games which occupy the minds of many young people.

"There is a perverse pleasure in watching others die because it's not me – it's them. I'm a survivor. This explains the dictator's mindset – the more people I kill, the more I am a survivor and the more powerful I feel."

He admits that fear of death is natural. "Fear of death is a very universal element in the human psyche. It's part of biological resistance to extinction, and also as human beings we are conscious of death in a way that seems other creatures are not and therefore our fear of death is something which quite naturally becomes repressed.

"Modern research suggests that the repression of the fear of death is actually our strongest and central repression, and in order to keep the fear of death out of sight, we construct security systems and value systems that reinforce that fear. Unfortunately, repression of anything as real as death causes a major dysfunction in our consciousness and behaviour and leads to the serious social phenomenon that we're witnessing."

He says the spiritual wisdom of all religious traditions has recognised that death is a reality of our life that has to be faced. "St Benedict says, for example, 'keep death always before your eyes.' He suggests that death has to be brought out of the shadows that are cast by repression, so that we can look it in the face.

"This is not to be morbid – in fact this is the opposite of morbidity, because the consciousness or mindfulness of death liberates us from the fear of death.

"I think many people who are in serious illness or facing mortality have discovered this – and many people in terminal illness have never known a better quality of life than in that last phase of their lives.

"A consequence of facing mindfulness of death is that we're able to deal with life, the losses of life and the separation that we have to experience in a more healthy, productive and constructive way – and we discover that we can grow through the necessary suffering of life."

Jesus, he says, shows us the way to view death. "Jesus was very aware of his own death and his mindfulness is a model for us, for his death was not a source of fear. He had a biological reaction, as we all do, but there was a voluntary acceptance of the laying down of his life. He was poised, centred and in touch with the process he was going through.

"He knew where he came from, and he knew where he was going to. He knew the Father, and that what he was doing was the will of the Father.

"Jesus was not afraid of death because death is not in God. God does not cease to love or care for us when we are dying or after death. God is deathless.

"The Christian understanding is that we can live without the fear of death. By dying Jesus broke the power of the devil – which was this fear of death."

So how does meditation help us to look death in the face? "Meditation is a dying that we accept and recognise as we let go of the immediacy of our desires and fears and thoughts. The little taste of death we experience in meditation helps us overcome our fear of death and see death as part of life and the growth process, and not just as the end of our physical body.

"Repeating the mantra (see box) is one way of dealing with the fear of death. When you say the mantra you are letting go of all fantasies and illusions and you are living in the present and entering the dying and rising of Christ.

"It is a process of coming into union with the mind of Christ and going with him, in him and through him to the ultimate goal which he describes as the Father."

....

For further information on Fr Laurence, Christian meditation or how to join a group visit www.wccm.org or www.christianmeditationaustralia.org

How to meditate

Sit down. Sit still and upright. Close your eyes lightly. Sit relaxed but alert. Silently, interiorly begin to say a single word. The prayer-phrase *Maranatha* is recommended. Say it simply – *ma-ra-na-tha* – as four equally stressed syllables. You can say the word in rhythm with your breathing, fairly slow, fairly rhythmical. Maranatha is Aramaic, the language Jesus spoke. It means 'Come, Lord.' It is probably the most ancient Christian prayer. It concludes 1 Corinthians and the Book of Revelation.

Listen to the mantra as you say it, gently and continuously. Do not think or imagine anything, spiritual or otherwise. Meditation is not quiet reverie or passive stillness, but attentive wakefulness. When thoughts or images come at the time of meditation they are distractions, so keep returning gently to saying your word. Don't try to dispel or repress distractions. Simply let them go by saying your word.

Meditate each morning and evening for between 20 and 30 minutes.

Entering into the space and stillness of icons

Icon writer Margaret Harper speaks to Roland Ashby about the spiritual power of icons. This interview appeared in the September 2012 edition of *TMA*.

Despite the apparent otherness and strangeness of icons, God can use them to convey his working, if we look at them patiently and not analytically and allow ourselves to be 'worked on', the Archbishop of Canterbury, Rowan Williams writes in *The Dwelling of the Light – Praying with Icons of Christ*.

This has certainly been Margaret Harper's experience, both as observer and icon writer (the technical term used for an icon painter).

Margaret, an Australian icon writer for nearly 10 years, told *TMA* that icons can sometimes be dismissed arrogantly as primitive, whereas their 'inverse perspective' reveals a high degree of sophistication. "If we're looking at a picture today, we expect to see a vanishing point receding into the picture, whereas in the inverse perspective used in icons, the vanishing point comes out to meet you and often goes beyond you, so that you are included in the picture and can walk into the scene."

This can have a profound effect on your understanding of the scene being described, Margaret says, who sees icons and icon writing as a form of prayer. "It's about entering a space, a stillness, not asking questions, not expecting anything in return, but just being able to open up and be there.

"It also takes you into a community of people stretching back centuries who have prayed in front of icons, and for whom they have been deeply significant."

During the many hours each icon takes to write, Margaret is drawn intimately into the scene, greatly moved by its significance.

"In writing the Icon of the Nativity, for example, I was filled with joy at the miracle of birth. Even though I understand the science of how it happens, this in no way explains the miracle of new life to me, both for humans and animals, let alone God and the miracle of the incarnation."

She also enjoys the icon's rich symbolism. "There is the coming out of the darkness of the cave into the light, and we are reminded of the importance of the symbolism of water in the Gospel by the inclusion of midwives washing the baby Jesus. This also speaks to me of Jesus' humanity and that this was a real baby who needed to be washed after birth."

When writing the Icon of the Crucifixion, she was also fascinated she says by the figure of Mary the Mother of Jesus. "One of the interesting features of Eastern representations of the crucifixion was what a strong figure the Mother of God is. She is standing there unsupported, she's not swooning into someone's arms. She's just standing there at the foot of the cross, able to bear this terrible sight of her son."

Margaret says she found the sadness of the Icon at times difficult to bear. "It's quite realistic with the blood running down the arms and over the feet. It was very hard to do as it arouses such strong feelings of sorrow.

"Before I started I did some research on crucifixion as a Roman punishment, and that was when I became aware of how truly appalling a tortured death it was, because you couldn't breathe, it was a very slow asphyxiation.

"That's partly why they put a foot pad on the cross – not for the comfort, but because if you could support your feet, you could breathe a bit longer."

Coming face to face with yourself – and God

The late Fr Michael King was the founding prior of St Michael's Priory, an Anglican Benedictine monastery in Camperdown, Victoria, Australia. Here he talks to Roland Ashby about living out the Rule of St Benedict, a short guide to the Benedictine life, written 1500 years ago by the founder of Western monasticism. The interview appeared in the July 2001 edition of *TMA*.

RA: The opening word of the Rule is 'Listen.'

MK: The listening is probably the most important thing about the whole of Benedict's Rule and the whole of the life of the monk or nun – the ability to listen in a world which by and large doesn't listen. We all come from a society which is dominated by noise. Not just the noises of machinery and traffic but the noises of people and the noises that we create for ourselves – our own inner noise.

I remember reading in the seventies a document by a community in Holland called *A Rule for a New Brother*, and they began the section on silence with these words: "You must bring to stillness the warring voices within your heart." Those words have stayed with me ever since because they relate very much to what Benedict is saying.

Benedict also says "Listen with the ear of your heart". Don't just listen externally, but listen with your whole being and listen to the precepts of your master. Listen to the words of the Lord. Listen to Scripture. Listen to the still small voice, remembering that through the silence we have an opportunity to actually create a situation where God may be present, or God may present Himself to us. I think that we spend the whole of our lives trying to master this listening process, because so much of our life is spent in the Divine Office or Liturgy of the Hours (seven communal prayer times each day, beginning with Vigils at 4.30 am and ending with Compline at 7.30 pm, in which the psalms are chanted and scripture read), and Lectio Divina, the meditative reading of Scripture.

Even in everyday conversation, when there are just two of us in dialogue, we often formulate what we are going to say next while the other person is speaking to us, and we are not really hearing what they are saying at all – we're working out what we're going to say! Benedict says, 'no, no, no. Listen with your whole being. Listen without trying to formulate an immediate response. Listen and be open to the way in which the Spirit of God draws you in.'

RA: Esther de Waal says God's presence can be seen, for example, in the Japanese tea ceremony, where the "most ordinary action and the most prosaic substance have become in that moment an act of worship". That seems to me to be the essence of what is meant by Benedictine 'listening.'

MK: Absolutely. I think that the wonderful thing about following any sort of divine spirituality is that it gives us the opportunity to place ourselves in the situation where through our listening we are able to allow God to make the most extraordinary out of the very normal. It's only when we are receptive to that listening process that we can begin to be a part of that action.

And there are so many ways in which God is present. God is present in all things, in every relationship. I think that we sometimes forget the omnipresence of God. We sometimes hide behind corners and think He can't really see me now, it's OK now. But it's not like that.

RA: So the monastery is a place of silence, but it is also a place of song. The Dominican Timothy Radcliffe says, "In this singing… we show forth God's bringing of everything to be… It is the beauty which celebrates the burst of creation."

MK: For Benedictines music is and has been an integral part of the Liturgy of the Hours and the celebration of the Eucharist from the very earliest times. The modern monastic chant that is used in a lot of communities today reflects the Gregorian modes and whilst it is a simpler chant it still conveys the joys and the sorrows.

But I think the music wills within us an act of praise. It brings from within a desire to express, to burst into song and to express our love for God and our joy and our redemption and the whole gamut of our salvation. St

Bernard said that he who sings well prays twice! I like St Bernard! It began for me in Melbourne's St Paul's Cathedral. I was a chorister aged 8-14.

RA: Balance between prayer and work is an important feature of the Rule. I think it's fairly true to say that many people struggle to find, or have lost, a sense of balance in their lives, particularly in relation to work.

MK: I think a lot of people today actually choose to overwork because it is an escape. It is an escape from the quietness and the solitude. You can do the same thing in the monastery. You can escape from reality by filling the day up with activity. Outside in the world a lot of people either consciously or unconsciously actually choose to be busy because it means they don't have to face themselves. They don't have to stand and look in the mirror and face reality, and so the activity becomes a sort of a cop-out from being a real person.

It is interesting with some people who are under-utilised within society how they also fill up their lives with activity. And then there are some people who don't, who actually savour the opportunity to have some space. A lot of the people who come to the guest house come simply for that reason – to have some space. People who live alone come and stay here and that always surprises me because they live alone, they live in solitude, so why do they want to come to a place like this? But it is a different sort of space.

Many people regard the monastic vocation as an escape from the world or as an escape from problems, but one has to realise that to fulfil a monastic vocation one has to be a complete person and one has to have faced life's problems and worked through them, because when you come into the monastery you are in fact forced to come face to face with yourself.

At the end of the day when you close the door on your cell it is as if you are in a room with four mirrored walls and all you see is who you are. If you are uncomfortable with that you won't last. What you have to see in that room with the four mirrored walls is the image of God: that is to say, yourself in the image of God.

RA: There are 12 steps of humility in the Rule. Timothy Radcliffe says again: "the climax of humility is when one discovers that not only is one not the centre of the world, but that one is not the centre of oneself." The two steps that really made me sit up are 1) you have to admit and be convinced that you are inferior to all and have less value than anybody else, and 2) you should be content with the lowest and most menial tasks. This is extremely counter-cultural!

MK: It is. The 12 steps of humility are really the basis of leading one into God and seeing oneself as in Christ. Here we are in a monastery where you have a definite hierarchical structure. And what is the Superior doing today? He's mowing grass. He's drying dishes. He is being an ordinary person and that's one of the beautiful things about our lives.

The whole thing about the sense of humility is that it is to bring us to the realisation of what our real worth is, and our real worth is in fact nothing, except that we are the redeemed, not just the monks but the whole of the Christian family.

RA: A most important part of becoming humble is being able to accept the call to obedience gladly, and again that is something that people probably find hard to accept today, because they equate being obedient with losing one's freedom or becoming subservient.

MK: I think that the obedience that we find in our vow of obedience is an obedience to be free. It is an obedience of joy and acceptance, that we joyfully accept God's will for us as shown through our observance of the Rule, through our reading and experience of Holy Scripture, through the teaching of Jesus and the guidance of the Community. And we certainly see our obedience as something that is mutual. It is obedience to one another as well as to the Abbot, but it is also obedience essentially to God and it is a joyful acceptance.

It's a bit like Mary's acceptance of the angel's greeting where he asked a few questions and there was a bit of hesitation, but she said 'well, here I am. I come to do your will'. It was the same with Jesus in his various conversations with the Father, particularly in the Garden of Gethsemane. It is the whole process of happily accepting that we freely give who we are and what we are to God with a joyful acceptance of His will for us.

There is a wonderful freedom about saying yes. If anyone has ever faced the situation where they have had to make an important decision in their lives and they have wrestled with it and they have come to a point of saying 'yes', they know something of this freedom too.

RA: There is also the requirement in the Rule to give up attachment to possessions, and at one point private ownership is described as an evil practice. So here is something else that is very confronting for a modern person.

MK: In the monastic community everything is everybody's, and yet one still gets people who yearn for ownership, and it is played out in various ways. People can have an area of responsibility and it becomes their possession, so there has to be a great care in not allowing that to take over. In larger communities than ours office bearers are changed regularly so that people don't become possessive about 'the kitchen' or 'the refectory'.

RA: Many people outside would devote a considerable part of their lives to acquiring possessions and working hard in order to get the sort of things they think they need or they ought to have.

MK: We have people who want us also to do that! They like to give us things in order to make us more like them. There have been occasions when we have had to say no, we don't need a DVD, or we don't need a computer, or we don't need a crystal jug and six goblets. There has to be a point where you recognise that we have what we need. We have necessary things, but we don't need to amass possessions or wealth.

RA: There is also the danger that many Westerners have really lost the sense of what is enough.

MK: Of course there is never enough. Because there is no cap to it there is never enough to actually satisfy. The satisfaction level always goes up, the desire goes up and it is never capped. I think that it is important that we live simply. Our vow of *conversio morum* really means don't be attached to people or possessions and be constantly turned around, be constantly converted.

RA: On a daily basis.

MK: Yes, absolutely. You have to say your yes every day and believe me we do! The whole thing about our vows – stability, obedience, *conversio morum* – they are all counter-cultural.

They say something though to the world. They say something about the ability to live in one place and be satisfied. They say something about being satisfied with God, and with God alone. Our conversion is a constant, not static. It keeps on changing and we keep on needing to be converted. And we are reminded of that each day in our prayer and our worship, of the need to turn around and to face God.

Our obedience is of course, if you like, the first rung of those three things – we begin with obedience, and our stability and our conversion are tempered with the obedience.

RA: "Forgiveness," according to Jean Vanier, "is the greatest fact of growth in the human being." The Rule says the Benedictine must always forgive and forbear. And there's to be no grumbling.

MK: One of the things that Benedict stipulates time and time again is that grumbling is the worst thing that can happen in community. By grumbling he means expressing one's dissatisfaction to others. Gossiping, talking about people behind their backs, all the sort of intrigue that goes on in communal groups, he says this is the most destructive thing and it mustn't happen.

If you have something to say, say it, but don't grumble about it, don't make murmurs. He calls it murmuring as well – there is to be no murmuring in the community.

And also with regard to anger and forgiveness, we mustn't let the sun set on our anger. We must always make our peace with our opponent. I think forgiveness in community is one of the most important factors of living together harmoniously – particularly the ability to forgive one another the little things. It is interesting that in community it is often not so much the big things that become issues, but the little ones.

RA: Hospitality is also an important aspect of the Rule, and the ability to see Christ in everyone.

MK: Benedict tells us that we must receive the stranger as Christ Himself, and particularly poor guests are to be appreciated more than the rich. He says the rich have enough appreciation of their own; it is in the poor in whom Christ particularly dwells. We are called to see Jesus in the person who presents himself to us – and that's sometimes not easy. It's not easy outside the monastery either.

All of the things incumbent upon us here in the monastery are also incumbent upon Christians out there in the world.

Contemplation the key to revival

Retired Anglican bishop Nigel McCulloch is credited with reversing the trend towards decline in the Diocese of Wakefield, in northern England, where he was bishop in the 1990s. He spoke to Roland Ashby when he was Bishop of Manchester for the June 2005 edition of *TMA* about the importance of prayer and contemplation as the starting point for renewal and evangelism.

Bishop Nigel McCulloch has never forgotten his first visit to Africa, when he sat at a function waiting for something to happen. After an hour of waiting he asked the bishop's wife next to him, "What are we supposed to do? Well, we wait," came the reply. "Eventually something did happen. But it was a little lesson in learning to slow down."

Bishop Nigel, who was born he says "ironically" on 17 January, the Feast Day of St Anthony of Egypt, the founder of monasticism, has sometimes been described he admits as "almost a workaholic". But it was while on a retreat he came to realise there was "a battle going on inside him between the busyness and the stillness". This is a "huge dilemma", he believes, "that affects all clergy in particular and not least bishops".

He tries to spend an hour each day in stillness and quiet, and have one quiet day each month and a week's retreat each year. "These are times of enormous richness and blessing. St Bernard said, 'If we are wise we will see life as a reservoir which retains the water until it is filled and then discharges the overflow without loss to itself. There are too many of us who pour out before we have been filled.'"

In these times of prayer and contemplation he has increasingly found the Anglican office of prayer "too wordy". He says it's important to find a space where he can be quiet and still, and begin by relaxing and breathing deeply. "You have really got to get the physical and breathing right because I think trying to find yourself in communion with God in a deeper way has about it a kind of musical aspect; in music rhythm is very important and there is a sense in which we have to be rhythmic to be able to draw closer to God."

Indeed, music, particularly Taize chants, plays a key part in his daily pattern of contemplation and prayer, both through the use of CDs and also through playing the chants over and over on the piano. He also takes a group of young people each year to the Taize community in France.

He often reads the psalms and "latches on to perhaps just a verse or even a phrase in a verse – and there has never been a day when at least a phrase or two has not come out off the page – and take that and use it almost in a kind of eastern, mantra style, just a concentration on beginning to make those few words real".

He says he has also found St Ignatius' style of "imaginative meditation" very helpful. "This is where you take a Bible story and place yourself in the positions of the different characters in the story. When you're actually in the mindset of a particular character you do really suddenly see things from a different angle."

As an aside he says he believes that if the Spanish spirituality of Ignatius' time (including the Carmelites John of the Cross and Teresa of Avila) had spread across Europe, "we would never have needed something like the Reformation. What they were trying to do was precisely what Luther and reformers were trying to do."

A sense of God's presence sometimes happens unexpectedly in his life. He recalls one particularly powerful time, when he felt a physical presence. "It was as if a big hand came onto my left shoulder and just pulled me back to just calm down and be still and know God."

While he acknowledges that such moments are rare, he does "hold on to them and to what you know to be the possibility of being in the presence of God in a way that is transfiguring, transforming."

These moments also sustain him through those "'dark night of the soul' periods which all of us go through, when we don't seem to be getting anywhere at all, and in fact seem to have gone badly backwards".

St Ignatius, he says, was very strong in believing "there isn't an absolute way that is right for each person, and that part of the value of imaginative meditation and getting into the mindset of other people is to realise that we all have different kinds of journeys, that our approaches to God are all different".

It's such an open and diverse approach to spirituality which he believes is likely to resonate with the postmodern unchurched interested in choice and individuality. And it's this reluctance to be too prescriptive which he argues is one of the strengths of Anglicanism at its best – "A generous tolerance and mutual respect – finding the mean between extremes – and drawing together under God differing views and diverse practices."

Its strength he adds is also an understanding of God expressed in the famous hymn by Fr Faber:
There is a wideness in God's mercy
For the love of God is broader than the measure of man's mind
And the heart of the eternal is most wonderfully kind
But we make his love too narrow by false limits of our own
And we magnify his strictness with a zeal he will not own.

He is concerned he says by the "puritan streak reasserting itself" in the Anglican Communion at the moment. "I think there is a negativity coming through, an almost unChristian disciplinarianism, which insists this is the way that it has to be done and then goes on beyond that to say 'and actually this isn't us thinking this, we know this is how God wants it.'

"The point about that hymn by Father Faber is to warn us against placing onto God our own particular values and distinctions."

He is also keen to dispel the myth that the Catholic wing of the Church isn't interested in evangelism. "There is a huge anglo-catholic tradition of great parish priests being out and about among people whom they knew they would never see in church at all. They knew their job was to incarnate the presence of the Lord in the situations where those people were.

"And in terms of worship, I know lots of catholic parishes where the symbolism and ritual are done in a sensitive way which enhances the worship wonderfully. The catholic movement has been using candles long before they were rediscovered by everyone else. There are so many little touches of symbolism and colour, which in our age of the visual medium, suggest that Catholicism has got it exactly right."

He is sceptical about the value of programs and training courses in evangelism. "The old phrase Christianity is caught, not taught, has a huge amount of truth in it. It is in the ordinary conversations, in the natural moments, when people can convey something of the genuineness of their faith, and so not appear to be trying to convert. This is what touches people and the little spark inside begins to come into a little flame."

When he was Bishop of Wakefield in the 1990s he realised the opportunity the approaching turn of the century presented for renewal and evangelism. In the 18 months leading up to the new millennium he visited each church in the diocese, first praying with anyone who wished to join him, then spending time alone with the clergy – "this was important because a lot of our clergy feel harassed, battered and embattled" – and finally he and the church would hold a "church in community reception", a service of preparation for the new millennium.

"My request was that we have about 60 people at the reception and the majority of them should not be church people. Everyone was invited at the service to come forward and receive a laying on of hands, and to have prayer said for them for their personal preparation and witness as we moved into the millennium.

"And I laid hands personally on just over 23,000 people during that time, a very powerful and humbling experience for me. But also I think for many it was quite a deep moment in their spiritual journey. There were lots of stories, including one I particularly remember, about a man who hadn't been to church for donkey's years. He approached me after the service with tears in his eyes. He had been confirmed at a service as a young lad in the army, but he had been so upset by the casual and impersonal way it had been conducted he felt cheated, and so hadn't had anything more to do with the Church since.

"It was decades later, at the laying on of hands at this service, that he felt that there had been a true confirmation moment. And I gather he is still going to church now.

"In helping people along their Christian journey it is so important for us to realise that the more personal we can be, the more we can convey the faith in personal terms, then the more likely we are to be able to present something of the individual love which the Saviour offers to us. And when we do that what we are doing is helping to create something infectious."

....

See 'Understanding Pope Francis' spirituality' in the Appendix.

Christendom over, faith enters a new era

Co-founder of the Christian Research Association (in Australia), Uniting Church Minister Dr Philip Hughes, who retired in 2016 after 30 years as its Director, spoke to Roland Ashby about why he believes the world has entered a new 'Axial Age'. The interview appeared in the September 2016 edition of *TMA*.

The Western Front of World War I was not only the scene of terrible carnage, it also marked the death of Christendom, says Philip Hughes. "For many Christians it was the end of their confidence in the whole idea that Christianity and civilisation were one and the same thing."

The Church, he believes, is facing another crisis of confidence today, under assault, as it is, on several fronts, including internally.

"Confidence in the Churches has dropped off significantly as a result of the sexual abuse scandals.

"A great external enemy of the Church has also been the rise of individualism, selfishness and greed that have been so effectively promoted by the corporate world, particularly through advertising, and also seen in recent corporate and banking scandals.

"Self-centred consumerism is rampant and has become faith's leading opponent in contemporary society. Faith calls us to reject this and says you will not find meaning ultimately by pursuing your own personal ends in this way."

Another stumbling block to faith he says has been the way science and faith often seem to be in conflict. "As a result, the whole story of belief is no longer credible to quite a large number of people."

However, he does not believe that the so called New Atheists have had a major impact in turning people away from faith. "It's interesting that almost all of the New Atheists are older men who tend to deal with the world of modernity rather than a postmodern world in which there are many truths and many ways of looking at truth. That's one of their great limitations."

Yet another significant factor in Church decline he says goes back to the 60s and 70s, and the new sexual freedom found through the contraceptive pill and the ensuing tendency for young people to live in de facto relationships.

"There was a huge drop in confidence in the Churches during this time, because they were seen to be out of step with this new freedom, and indeed, inhibitors of progress.

"When young people moved into de facto relationships they recognised they were moving outside the norms of the Christian Churches. Many left the Church as a result."

He believes the Church's perceived narrowness and lack of tolerance for diversity undermined its moral authority, something which has been further exacerbated by the Church's lack of leadership on other important moral issues of the day such as sustainability of the environment.

"This, together with the Church's cover ups of sexual abuse, has therefore led many to view the Churches as moral failures."

But perhaps the greatest underlying challenge – and opportunity – for the Church is what Dr Hughes calls a new "Axial Age".

"The Axial Age was a term coined to describe the period 700-450 BC in which there was the rise of prophet-like figures in all of the major civilisations of the time; Confucius in China, Buddha in India, Jeremiah and other prophets in Israel, Socrates and Plato in Greece. Religion moved from being something that was primarily about honouring the gods, to something which was also about living morally with each other.

"It was a huge leap in the nature of religion, and it seems to me we are part way through an age in which there is a shift in the nature of religiosity of a similar size."

Religion in this new Axial Age, he believes, is not so much about what you believe, as what you experience. "It's an Age in which what is most important is how you feel in relation to God; your experience of God. So the nature of worship is changing too. We are moving from something which is very rational to something which is very experiential."

It is an Age in which many would describe themselves as "spiritual but not religious" he says, "which at its heart is the sense that your spirituality is an individual thing which is owned by the individual. The individual becomes the reference point for its content, nature and resourcing, rather than being a big communal thing which is actually owned and governed by the institution."

Their spirituality, he says, "is often either an eclectic mix drawn from a wide variety of sources, including Buddhism and yoga, or it is based around the environment and nature".

The future Church he believes will consist of either mega-churches or "boutique" churches. "There are increasing numbers attending the big mega-churches. At the moment, of all non-Catholics who attend a church in Melbourne, 20 per cent attend two per cent of the churches. So that trend is very clear.

"The other trend is towards boutique churches which cater for particular ethnicities, interests, or forms of music and worship.

"Those churches that best meet their members' needs and interests, and provide a place of community and belonging, tend to be the most vibrant."

He suggests that one way for older congregations to attract younger members would be to start groups or activities around their interests. "Our recent surveys of young people show that there are many who aren't interested in worship, but are interested in being part of a music or drama group, or becoming involved in a social justice group or activity, and in fact there are many who are involved in those things who don't come to worship.

"Let's open those doors to create a variety of pathways, rather than expecting that all are going to find their expression of faith through the worship service on Sunday morning."

After 30 years of witnessing the diminution of Christian influence on the culture generally, he is concerned about what this might mean for the future. "I am disappointed, for example, that our government schools have increasingly become no-go areas in terms of values and the whole sense of the meaning and purpose of life". Yet there are continuing positive areas of influence, he believes. "Many church-related schools do address values and the creation of meaning and purpose in life. Church-related social welfare organisations also have the capacity to add value to welfare, and many church-based social justice activities contribute to creating a better society. Moreover, many parishes provide nurture and support as well as creating communities in which people find fulfilment through serving others."

Dr Hughes' latest book, Charting the Faith of Australians – Thirty Years in the Christian Research Association, *is available from the Christian Research Association website: http://cra.org.au/products-page/books/charting-the-faith-of-australians-thirty-years-in-the-christian-research-association/.*

Ray Simpson (L) and Brent Lyons-Lee

Call from God leads to global Celtic fellowship

Anglican priest Ray Simpson, who received what he believes was a call from God to found a global community inspired by the Celtic saints Aidan and Hilda, and Australian member of the Community, Baptist minister Brent Lyons-Lee, speak to Roland Ashby about their book *Celtic Spirituality in the Australian Landscape*. The interview appeared in the June 2015 edition of *TMA*.

At midnight on New Year's Eve 1987, Anglican priest Ray Simpson received what he believes was a call from God. He was staying on the ancient Celtic Christian island of Lindisfarne on England's north-east coast.

"After watching the then Archbishop of Canterbury's New Year message on the importance of cradle places in bringing faith to nations, I switched off the TV, knelt down in pitch darkness and offered myself to God. I then had a very, very powerful sense that God was saying, with unmistakeable clarity, 'I want my people to rediscover my presence in creation, among people in the streets from all backgrounds, and in the unseen world of saints and angels; I want them to travel light, to strip away the excess baggage they have accumulated over the centuries, and to make a space in their hearts for hospitality to others.'"

Ray had been searching for a way to bring the different streams of Christianity together in a way that was both contemplative and active in the world, and believes the holy isle of Lindisfarne was being called anew to be a cradle place for a revitalised Christianity inspired by its Celtic heritage, and so he became the founding Guardian of the Community of Aidan and Hilda. In the seventh century, St Aidan set up a monastic community on Lindisfarne, and served as the region's first bishop, and St Hilda established a monastery in nearby Whitby.

The Community of Aidan and Hilda is now an ecumenical worldwide fellowship, which has a small retreat house and study library at Lindisfarne. It seeks to "reconnect with the Spirit and the Scriptures, the streets and the saints, the seasons and the soil, to heal the land and resource churches to become holistic community hubs". It also has its own 'three R's': "Rhythm with God, Roots in the land, Relationship with the people."

Ray told *TMA* that the Community had been named after Aidan and Hilda because of the love, grace and wisdom they showed in helping to bring Christianity to the north of England.

"St Aidan, whose name means Little Flame, was a monk from Iona, the monastery established by St Columba on Scotland's west coast. His approach to mission was very different from the Roman tradition. He wore simple woollen clothing, gave donations to the poor and refused to ride a horse because that would have put him above people; only landowners and warriors had horses.

"He and his fellow monks learned the scriptures and psalms by heart and meditated on them as they walked. He also taught his brothers, when they met someone, to befriend them, and once they had established a relationship to share the Gospel with them. The people loved him. He said what they needed was milk – the milk of kindness, the milk of Christ."

"Hilda was a remarkable leader. She was known for her mercy and wisdom, and I believe that one of the great things about her was that she retained her integrity when the Synod of Whitby decided on a Roman, rather than Celtic, framework for the Church."

The Community of Aidan and Hilda seeks to live by monastic principles of finding a balance between prayer and work in daily life, and seeing work as giving expression to God-given creativity and as a way of serving and praising God.

It has also adopted the vows of simplicity, purity and obedience (a variation on the traditional monastic vows of poverty, chastity and obedience).

"Bonhoeffer said 'The restoration of the Church must surely come from a new kind of monasticism'", says Ray. "The call to simplicity is rooted in Jesus' beatitude 'Blessed are the poor in spirit'. It's a daily attention to letting go of the 'excess baggage' – and anything we're attached to such as possessions or status.

"Purity is about living out of the love of the source of all of us – God. So, if our work is pure it's because we're not doing it to get rich or please an employer; we're doing it ultimately for God, as far as we're able, and to serve others.

"Purity is also about asking those in sexual relationships not to treat sex as a cheap commodity, but to show deep respect for the other person.

"And with obedience we often link it to the Rublev Icon of the Trinity; in which the three persons of the Trinity are looking not to their own interest but to the interest of others, humbly serving; and because they trust the others they know that they will not be abused. So it's not subservience. I think the three vows add up to a very beautiful way of living life."

Contemplation – daily prayer, meditation and silence – as well as a commitment to a "deep spirituality that transforms the root evils of society" are also essential "waymarks", or guiding principles, of the Community; and each member is also invited to find a "soul friend".

"A soul friend is a spiritual director who accompanies you on your faith journey, who is a good listener, reflects a lot on Scripture and is familiar with different ways of prayer," explains Ray.

Brent Lyons-Lee, who spent more than 10 years with Urban Seed at Collins Street Baptist Church in Melbourne, says the Australian members are exploring what an Australian Indigenous expression of the Aidan and Hilda tradition looks like.

"Maybe our thin places [Celtic sacred places where heaven and earth seem to meet] are places like Uluru and similar places where we can find God in creation.

"In the book we also recognise the connections between Celtic and Aboriginal Spirituality – the importance of silence and intuition, and interconnectedness between each other and the land. One of the common threads is what Indigenous Australians in Southern Queensland called *Dadirri* – a deep listening for the presence of the 'great Life-Giving Spirit'. As the Aboriginal writer Miriam-Rose Ungunmerr-Baumann explains, 'Dadirri brings wholeness by enjoying the land, being attentive to the seasons… being together for ceremonies, listening to sacred stories and being at home in silence and in God's presence'".

....

Celtic Spirituality in the Australian Landscape, *by Ray Simpson and Brent-Lyons Lee, is published by Saint Aidan Press. For more information about the Community of Aidan and Hilda see www.aidanandhilda.org.au*

Healing the 'father wound' in men's psyches

Pastor Richard Fay was furious with God after he experienced a breakdown in his 40s, but then he attended a men's retreat and discovered his 'father wound'. He now leads an annual five day retreat for men called Men's Rites of Passage which helps men to prepare for the second half of life. He spoke to Roland Ashby. The interview appeared in the May 2015 edition of *TMA*.

RA: You have written that you've met very few men who have reached manhood without a 'father wound'. As we commemorate World War I, we are perhaps more aware than we used to be of the psychological harm that war inflicts on those who return.

RF: We had 60,000 men die in World War I, but we had 200,000 maimed and that is the physical maiming. We cannot measure the psychological maiming. My grandfather was an artilleryman in France and he never once mentioned the War, not once. My father was the same. He would not speak about his experience in Papua New Guinea in the Second World War. Neither of them would march, get together with their mates from the war or talk about it. They wanted to get on with life, they wanted to leave it behind; but I know that they could not.

My own 'father wound' is not so much from war, but from circumstances. My grandmother died giving birth to my father. It was her first child and she bled out over 36 hours. My grandfather was a young man and he remarried in haste and grief; he was alone in the world with a son and not knowing how to raise a son. But he was still in love with the wife that he had lost and his second wife knew this, and I suspect anything that represented that first marriage she felt uncomfortable with, and my father was the one constant reminder.

They had two children and my father was not allowed in that family home; he was raised by his grandmother and eventually by a single aunt. So he ended up being a deeply wounded man and, being his only son, I reminded him of his own unresolved pain. He went to church, but in the home, in my own experience, he could not show safe presence and strong love. He did for my very early years, but once I reached the middle primary years, that's when the distance and aloofness began.

RA: You reached a point in your late 40s when you became, you say, furious with God. What happened?

RF: Believing in a transactional God, I expected him to fulfil his end of the bargain if I fulfilled my end. I served him faithfully as a pastor only to find myself in burnout, in depression, without answers to some of the stickiest things in my own life – some of the deep underlying psychological malaise that came from my relationship with my father and undigested psychological material. I thought God would have shifted those things and it was clear that he wanted to use different methods. He isn't a transactional God, he's a relational God.

RA: You quote Carl Jung who said we are thoroughly unprepared for the 'afternoon of life'. What is it in the second half of life that we need to prepare for and how do we begin? You say this is a period of transition that we need to be initiated into.

RF: There's a recognition that happens at sometime between the ages of 40 to 50 for most men that life is not going to get better; the body starts going south, the kids start finding their own worlds and so suddenly you're an empty-nester; the career trajectory won't get much better than this if at all – in fact it will probably slowly diminish and then end. So the path is one of letting go, of surrendering and trusting, and that's counter-intuitive to a man's first half of life, which is achieving, proving himself, building an identity based on his career, based on his ability to perform and make stuff happen.

RA: You say that many men who don't conform to expectations of success experience a primary underlying emotional shame.

RF: Primary, yes, but that doesn't mean that a man will admit to it. It's an emotion that's too awful to face square-on because it violates his identity. But if you asked him about anger, frustration or resignation, possibly even despair and addiction, those things he'll know. He will use these secondary emotions to cover it up. If he is ashamed of who he is – unconsciously, not consciously – then he will continue to act out in one of those ways.

RA: You say we've become divorced from some ancient wisdoms. What are they?

RF: For example, the way that Indigenous people would initiate their boys. The men would take the boys away from the community, paint them white from head to toe – white being the colour of death – then send them out into the desert on their own. To be disconnected, separated from your community is death. They would wander alone and be reminded constantly in these surroundings that they are not in control, they are not important and it's not about them; that this life is incredibly hard – where am I going to find water? Where am I going to find food? – and that they're going to die. They would look at the stars, the heavens, and they would realise their insignificance and place in this great cosmos. Eventually they're welcomed back by the men and celebrated into manhood. Adolescence lasts about a week.

White Australians said they were primitive and our ways were better. We've forgotten these things so we say to a boy you are important, not that you are part of something great. We do not believe that we are going to die because we take death and put it in a clinical place away from our lives and we even put ageing in a place where we don't see it. Sadly all the wisdom is taken from us when we do that. We say we are in control, we western white men: my goodness, look at the great machinery and sophistication and technology that we keep on building! Even though it seems to be bringing devastation to our planet we can do it; but we do not know that we are not in control.

RA: What are some of the key elements of the Retreat?

RF: The power of dream and symbol, fire, connecting with nature, drumming together, silence, solitude and poetry are all important elements.

We notice that our dreams come to us symbolically because our ego is turned off when we go to sleep and often it's telling us deep unconscious truths.

Fire is a metaphor for God so often in the Bible. You can't define its form because it's constantly changing, and on a dark night, particularly when it's cold, with the heat pulsing from the fire, the flames dancing before you, it mesmerises, it fascinates. It draws you in so you can find something to focus on that's beyond yourself and in that place, with shadows dancing, and your own shadow in the light, you are able to share some of your deeper secrets safely.

We learn to pay attention to nature and recapture a sense of its beauty and wonder because we've become urbanised, disconnected from it.

Many men I speak to punch holes through walls in frustration or kick something over, but with drumming it's a healthy use of this masculine energy; and when the rhythm starts there's a connection with all the men because we're all following and joining. It's just as simple as that. It allows a man to express himself physically in a way that's fun and rhythmic and it binds us together.

I heard it said, from the fairly conservative background I came from, don't go into silence because that's where the devil comes in. I want to agree with that because when Jesus went into silence, that's where his three temptations in the wilderness came from. But those three temptations must be faced and if we don't face them then we will act out of them. In their book *Principles of Trauma Therapy* psychologists John Briere and Catherine Scott say that anything we cannot hold we will not process and whatever we do not process haunts us, and so we are haunted by that which we do not face. Silence is the place where you can no longer run from it.

In silence you can become present to God's love for you, by silently repeating a simple sacred word with your breath such as Jesus or Abba. As you breathe in you breathe in His love, and as you breathe out you let go of your frustration or anxiety. You also become aware of how you mostly identify with your thoughts. They snare you. You attach to them. They reinforce a whole lot of energy within you which is not healthy and they're often about the past or the future. So you are never actually present to here and now. Silence starts to dislodge all of those control mechanisms. It loosens the grip of our ego so that we move to a place of surrender, a place of trust, a place of not so much where prayer is about loving God as it is about being loved by God. Silence then becomes the most beautiful invitation, a living sacrament, a place you can dwell and delight in.

Writing poetry is also a part of the retreat. It's a beautiful way of finding language for our souls, to describe truths that cannot be told through rational means. Again, poetry has become a lost art but I think there is a resurgence of interest. You can read a poem for years and find comfort and deeper meaning from it.

RA: Apart from Christian meditation what other elements of Christian spirituality are introduced in the retreat?

RF: We draw on Scripture in powerful ways, such as chanting passages from 1 Corinthians 13 and adapting them in a way that will be remembered: 'When I was a boy, I thought as a boy. Now I am a man, I live as a man'.

We make the cross of Christ the central element of the retreat because we know that unless we go through our suffering and accept death, the death of all things, we will not be transformed. We cannot simply jump to the resurrection, to Easter Sunday morning and hope for bright, shiny things. We have no control over salvation, over healing, over transformation; we can only give ourselves to God that it might happen and it will happen as He wills, not as we will.

RA: I'm sure a lot of people would be curious to know why the retreat is gender-specific.

RF: One of the reasons is that men process pain differently from women. Women may weep. Men may get very angry. That can intimidate women. Many men aren't immediately relational. We can be relational, but our approach is different, it's not as direct.

Women have historically started with nurturance and with relationship and have had to find their own ascension later in life. Men have started with ascension and need to learn their own descent. Often at the very time that a woman is ascending, the man is descending, in the sense that the man is having to let go; but the woman is now invited to step up, and it happens often in the 40s and 50s.

RA: How do you believe that men in particular should be formed for ministry?

RF: There is still not enough emphasis on psychological formation. Men who train for the ministry need to be aware of their shadow, they need to be aware of their use of power, and their motivations for seeking profile, importance or prominence. And, of course, worst of all, if they are seeking to find security then there'll be no true mission heart, there'll be no risk-taking.

See www.centreformenaustralia.org.au/events/mens-rights-of-passage/

Letting in the Self that comes to us from God

A Rhodes Scholar who studied under Rowan Williams, Dr Sarah Bachelard left the church for many years before returning after a 'moment of grace'. She talks to Roland Ashby about her journey from 'dis-integration to healing' and her book *Resurrection and Moral Imagination*, which explores the power of the resurrection to transform the way we see the world. The interview appeared in the September 2014 edition of *TMA*.

Sarah Bachelard begins *Resurrection and Moral Imagination* with a wonderful story that Australian philosopher Raimond Gaita tells about his experience as a ward assistant in a psychiatric hospital at the age of 17.

Even though some of the psychiatrists were devoted to improving the lives of their patients, and obviously believed in their "inalienable dignity", as he describes it, he was greatly struck by the visit of a nun one day and her love for the patients, which had such a different quality from the psychiatrists' love. He reflected, Sarah writes, that "what was astonishing about the nun's love for the patients was its power to reveal what their affliction had obscured, the power to reveal their full humanity and moral equality".

Here is a love, Sarah believes, that is made possible if we allow the risen Christ to become the new horizon of our lives. "If the resurrection is the horizon of our lives and we become open to God as infinitely loving and merciful, that's going to make a difference to how we live and see others and ourselves," she says.

Pope Francis said in his first encyclical this is about seeing others as God sees them and having a faith which is understood: "When we receive the immense love of God which transforms us inwardly and enables us to see reality with new eyes."

"There is something about the love of God which is able to let the other fully be itself, is able to let the other be," Sarah says. "We no longer feel threatened by others, compare ourselves to them, compete with them or define ourselves over against them."

If we want to see in this way, she says we need to have "a transparency to God's love", an openness to becoming a channel of God's love. "It's about letting go of the false self, the ego, with its endless schemes, agendas, judgements and self-justifications, and letting in the Self that somehow comes to us from God. This is what it means to be 'pure in heart' as in 'Blessed are the pure in heart, for they shall see God.'"

For this to happen, she says, "a stripping away" of the illusory self, a self-forgetfulness, is required, so that you "realise where you have always been, which is grounded in God. It's just that a sense of alienation or separation is in the way."

But this is no easy or comfortable process, Sarah explains. "We are called to go beyond the consolations of religion into the fierce presence of the living God. We have to experience a 'dis-integration' and a wounding before we can experience healing and integration. Rowan Williams says that our healing 'lies in obedient acceptance of God's will; but this is no bland resignation. It is a change wrought by anguish, darkness and stripping.'"

Sarah's 'dis-integration' – and healing – began during a 10-year period in which she had left the church. "About 15 years ago, when I was doing my PhD, I got to the point where I suddenly felt 'I can't do it.' I was three years in and I was nowhere near having a thesis, and this wave of panic came over me and I was convinced I was going to fail."

Despite being constantly "consumed by anxiety," she went on to complete the doctorate. However, because the anxiety remained and she continued to feel that she was always "standing on the edge of an abyss", she decided to attend a course in personal development.

"It was here that I was confronted with a view of myself that I realised I had developed at the age of five – that I was inadequate – and I suddenly saw that wasn't true.

"I suddenly had this experience of profound self-acceptance, and just saw all the ways in which my whole life I had been desperately trying to make up for this supposed lack. Then, pretty quickly after that, I had this profound experience of acceptance of and love for people because I saw that we're all doing that, we are all trapped in that.

"So that was a moment of grace, a conversion experience, a freedom from this ancient pattern. For the first time loving others was not something I *should* do, it wasn't the moral imperative, it was just that when you stripped everything away what you ended up with was love.

"And then I arrived at the extraordinary thought that, for all the ways it betrays this and fails to embody this, the Church exists as a public institution in our world to say, 'That is what it's about.'"

Sarah returned to the Church, which "stopped being unsatisfactory wallpaper", and was delighted to discover Christian meditation. She joined the World Community for Christian Meditation and is now its Australian Youth Co-ordinator. "I had been meditating in the Buddhist way with the breath, but it was very exciting for me to discover through WCCM a meditation practice that was in concert with my Christian theological understanding."

She was ordained priest in the Anglican Church in 2006 and has recently begun a contemplative church called Benedictus, an ecumenical worshipping community which meets in Cook in the ACT.

"Benedictus offers worship times characterised by simplicity, silence and non-distractedness and which seek to integrate reflection on Scripture with contemplative prayer.

"Its aim is to offer a transformative journey and help people who are serious about making that journey."

For further information about the World Community for Christian Meditation see: www.wccm.org
www.christianmeditationaustralia.org
For Benedictus contemplative church,
see: www.benedictus.com.au

Photo credit: Kathy Luu

'Christianity gave us a divine sense of our equality'

Australian Indigenous journalist Stan Grant talks to Emma Halgren about the "deep stain" of racism towards Indigenous Australians, and how Christianity has had a positive impact, despite its association with the negative effects of colonialism. The interview appeared in the April 2016 edition of *TMA*.

Australia still lacks the creative and courageous leadership it needs for its Indigenous people to be included in "the greatness that is Australia", says Stan Grant – and Indigenous people are suffering today as a result of a longstanding racism in Australia that is "a deep, deep stain on the soul of the nation".

In an interview with *TMA*, Stan Grant said that decades of purposeful nation-building had failed to include Indigenous people.

"You don't build a country like Australia by accident," he said. "When I look around Australia I see what it has created.

"It has created this extraordinary, prosperous, tolerant, free, democratic, safe, secure society – but not for us. And the hope is that the greatness of Australia is going to be also applied to us."

He said that he had been appalled by what he saw as a muted response to the suicide of a 10-year-old girl in Western Australia in March, an event that he says should have been as much of a wake-up call to Australians as the death of young Syrian boy Aylan Kurdi on a Turkish beach in September last year was to the world.

"We could see ourselves in that boy," he said. "We could see ourselves in the tragedy of that death. We could see ourselves in the humanity of the struggle of people to find safe havens from war. But why can we not see ourselves in the death of that poor little girl?

"That should be our defining moment; that should be the moment at which we say 'this is enough, this is a collective failure, a failure of us as a nation, a failure of our policies'. And for Indigenous people as well, to look at ourselves and say 'we failed too'.

"And what have I heard since? Just a deafening silence… a failure to grapple with it, a failure of comment from our leaders. I haven't heard the outrage in the media, I haven't heard from our Prime Minister or our Opposition Leader."

He said he was dismayed by the way politicians seemed to "shrug off" Indigenous issues or consign them to the sphere of socially progressive causes.

"We sit off to one side… when we should be at the centre of political debate, alongside the hard questions of taxation reform or immigration policy or health policy," he said.

"This failure to see Indigenous affairs as integral to the well-being of this nation has just let us down."

In October 2015, Grant gave a speech at the Ethics Centre in Sydney in which he claimed that the "Australian dream" was "rooted in racism". He said, "It is the very foundation of the dream. It is there at the birth of the nation. It is there in *terra nullius*."

Still today, he said, "racism is killing the Australian dream".

"My people die young in this country. We die 10 years younger than average Australians… We are fewer than three per cent of the Australian population and yet we are 25 per cent – a quarter – of those Australians locked up in our prisons. And if you're a juvenile it is worse, it is 50 per cent. An Indigenous child is more likely to be locked up in prison than they are to finish high school."

Christianity gave 'greater sense of our rights'
Stan Grant told *TMA* that Christianity had played an "extraordinarily important" part in his and his family's life.

"Christianity and the missions that were set up around New South Wales, Victoria, helped give birth to the beginnings of the Aboriginal political movement," he said.

"The fights for citizenship and equality came directly out of that Christian experience. Men and women… emerged from the missions with a divine sense of their equality. My grandfather was one of them. He went away to fight a war for this country when he wasn't even a citizen. He came back to this country where we're segregated and his basic human rights were denied.

"But he believed in his divine right, the divine right of his own humanity and his equality and he fought for that. God had told him you are an equal and he demanded that equality from Australia."

He said that while Christianity's impact was certainly not all positive – "the Christianising was often coupled with civilising… we saw the destruction of culture, the denial of tradition, the silencing of language" – Indigenous people had been able to take its core messages and be empowered by them.

"It helped give rise to a greater sense of our rights and our equality and our humanity, and I'm directly shaped by that. I remember going to the mission church near where I lived and my uncle preaching stories about overcoming oppression. We took the Christian message and like the black American churches did, turned it into a potent political message of survival and salvation and equality."

He said that although he did not now locate himself within a particular faith, he had a "very, very strong spiritual belief and sense of the importance of spirituality to our lives… I've seen it work in people's lives, I've seen the impact it can have."

In his new book, *Talking to My Country*, Stan Grant reflects on race and national identity, and his own experience of growing up as an Indigenous person in Australia.

He said his goal with the book was simple: to encourage non-Indigenous Australians to "see us as human beings. See in our lives, your life. See how we've lived with the full weight of this history. See how this has shaped the malaise that sits so heavily a part of Indigenous communities and Indigenous life.

"It's a very, very simple story. It's the story of people, of lives, shaped by the weight of our country's history, and I think if anyone comes to it with an open mind and an open heart, they couldn't help but see the humanity of that story."

....

Emma Halgren is Deputy Editor of TMA and a freelance writer and editor. She has worked for more than 15 years in communications in not-for-profit and church organisations in Sydney, Geneva and Melbourne. She has studied politics, journalism and theology.

The end of Christendom a great opportunity

In 2001 *Time* magazine named Stanley Hauerwas as 'America's Best Theologian'. The prolific author and Professor Emeritus of Divinity and Law at Duke Divinity School, North Carolina, speaks to Roland Ashby about why he is not despairing about the demise of Christendom – or about death. The interview appeared in the March 2014 edition of *TMA*.

Christendom in the West is approaching its end, but this is a good thing, Stanley Hauwerwas believes. "Christendom is the time when being a Christian is an advantage. We're moving into a time when being a Christian is not an advantage, and that means that those people who discover that they're Christian will have to be very serious about that. So the loss of Christendom is a great opportunity for the Church to become a more disciplined community."

As the Church struggles to survive and adapt, he predicts that it will increasingly become "a community of people who need one another, just in order to survive, and therefore friendship will become increasingly precious for such a community. And that will be a wonderful witness to the world."

At age 73, he recognises too that he is approaching a time when "death is no longer just a theoretical possibility." "I thought I would fear death, but as yet I haven't found that to be the case. I keep a poem above my desk which asks 'Why fear that door where so many friends have gone?' Although we do not know what it might mean to be a citizen of heaven after death, I have every confidence that God cares, and I look forward to discovering what that might mean."

Although he rejects the notion that the dead go to a 'better place', because "God is not a place" he told *TMA* that he thinks of being with God after death "as simply being part of absolute glory, just being captivated by a beauty so overwhelming you don't think about yourself".

I asked him to explain why being a Christian "has not and does not come naturally or easily for me". "For some people God is just there, but God is not just there for me," he replies. "I have learnt to find God in the lives of others."

God is particularly present for him, he says, in the poor. "It's primarily being with mentally disabled people. People don't normally think of them as poor, but they have a vulnerability because they have no way to protect themselves from harm, and I think that's the way we all are but fail to acknowledge it. I find people that have nothing to lose just have a more straightforward way of saying that God makes life possible in a way that I can't say, and so I find their testimony extremely powerful.

"I love the social activist Dorothy Day who established the Catholic Worker Movement. She was just wonderful. Jean Vanier, Founder of the L'Arche communities for the disabled, is my deepest exemplar. I'm also so impressed by a couple I know whose lives have been transformed by having a mentally disabled child, and whose lives are joyful. Ordinary people are just remarkable in the witness that they oftentimes enact for those of us who've never really had to suffer much."

He is full of admiration too for the members of his own (Anglican) church who over a 15-year period have committed themselves to working with Haitians to assist them with a rebuilding project.

Churches must offer an alternative vision of society, and a distinctive way of being, he says, in which "their first task is not to make the world more just, but to make the world the world," by which he means, "the world cannot know it is the world unless there's a group of people offering an alternative to the world."

The church will be a community of people whose "charter is the Gospel of Jesus Christ", living out of the conviction that the 'powers and principalities' that St Paul refers to have been defeated in the cross. "You also see these powers defeated in Jesus' temptation narrative in Luke – the powers of money, political power and the belief that we need to use violence to do good."

In an echo of Pope Francis he says that churches must also be "communities of poor that care for the poor." "To be Christian is to be obligated to be charitable, and care for the poor cannot be separated from the worship of God... Self-sacrificial giving to the poor is sacramental. We meet Christ in acts of mercy, and we must learn that to be reliant on God is not only to learn how to give to the poor, but be *with* the poor. We need to befriend them as God has befriended us.

"The most important thing we have to give to the poor is God. We come bearing the gift of Christ."

This is the love "manifest in Christ's life, death and resurrection," he writes in his memoir *Hannah's Child*, and it is "God's unrelenting desire for us to want to be loved by that love."

As in the Road to Emmaus story, he says we are not good at recognising the Risen Christ, "because we tend to be just admirers, rather than disciples, of Christ".

In a world obsessed with speed, busyness and distraction, discipleship more than ever, he maintains, requires a disciplined prayer life (he rises at 4.30am each morning to pray), silence and patience. "Christians must be formed to resist speed."

In his 2013 book *Approaching the End*, he writes, "If I could choose any epigraph that might summarise what my work has been about it would be 'Keep your mind in hell and despair not.'"

"Hell", he explains, "is the isolation from God and one another" which characterises much of life today. "To keep our minds in this place and not to despair requires that we really know that God has not abandoned us."

Mission not about 'scalp-hunting' for Jesus

Mission must not be anxiety-driven, must resonate with people's needs and longings, and must witness to the love and joy of Christ, says Stephen Cottrell, Bishop of Chelmsford, a leading missioner in the Church of England who found working in a hospice for the dying transformed his understanding of ministry. He spoke to Roland Ashby for the September 2015 edition of *TMA*.

When he was a little boy, before he went to sleep at night, Stephen Cottrell's mother would tell him that if all the little boys of the world were lined up and she was given a choice about which one to choose, she would choose him. "And when I was bad-tempered she dealt with it by holding me and hugging me, until the rage had subsided. Not only was I healed, I was transformed in love."

It is the same with God, he says. "He shows wonderful affirmations of love. He says 'I hold you, I choose you, I long for you, my heart flames with compassion and love for you.'"

Bishop Cottrell tells congregations the reason they are in church is God's great love for each of them in Jesus Christ. "Jesus became the one who holds us. Think of him with his arms outstretched on the cross. Through him God is saying 'I want to hold you and go on holding you'... with the crucifixion we see what love looks like when it goes on loving."

Prayer, for him, is about connecting with this love. "Prayer is the lover coming into the presence of the beloved and saying 'I love you', and by 'lover' I mean God, the great lover who comes to me and says 'I love you' and through the affirmation of that love I am changed; my will is united with Christ. My times of prayer and contemplation are fundamentally about opening up to God's love."

Bishop Cottrell said mission is powerfully illustrated by the story of the little boy, "who after hearing the priest in his sermon say Jesus must live in your heart, afterwards asked the priest, 'Jesus is so big and I am so small, so if Jesus came to live in my heart, wouldn't he burst out all over the place?' and the priest replied, 'Yes, that's how it works'".

"Mission flows out of this 'abundant heart' – living joyfully and sharing profligately the Good News of Jesus Christ. We also need to remember the first words spoken by the risen Jesus (to Mary Magdalene in St John's Gospel): 'Why are you weeping?'

"Mission shouldn't be anxiety-driven and it's not about 'scalp hunting for Jesus'. Evangelism isn't about converting people. That's God's job. God is the missionary and the Holy Spirit is the evangelist. My job is to be, first of all, a living signpost. Each of us needs to ask: In what sense is my life a signpost to Christ? When people meet me, do they, in any sense, encounter Jesus Christ?

"Secondly, every Christian is called to be a good companion – to walk alongside others, to listen and serve.

"Only God can convert. Conversion is a sacred mystery and it's about the free response of the human spirit to what God has done in Jesus Christ. All I can do is bear witness to it, to point to it."

Mission is also about seeing – and acting on – opportunities to witness to it. "For example, I was having coffee at a café last week and overheard two young guys in their 20s at the next table. They were talking about why the fish is a Christian symbol; they had no idea and were putting forth various theories. After a minute or two I said, 'look, excuse me, I can't help but hear your conversation', and I explained the significance of the symbol.

"Now there are people who are growing up in a culture where they know very little about the Christian faith. They've probably never been to church, and in a funny kind of way, when the culture reaches that stage, the Christian faith actually becomes quite an interesting novelty, and I think that's the stage we're moving into.

"Previous generations knew just enough Christianity to be kind of vaccinated. We kind of successfully inoculated the culture against the Christian faith by giving people just a little bit of it – and then they're immune for the rest of their lives! Now many know nothing and, in knowing nothing, don't have nearly as much hostility as some people think they have."

Young people, he believes, tend to be more interested in the question 'does it work?' than 'is it true?'. "Their questions are: What difference does it make to my life? How does it equip me for life? How does it satisfy my longing for self-realisation and self-fulfilment? And whereas quite often in previous generations our evangelism was doctrine-led, my hunch is in the current culture it needs to be spirituality-led."

Effective mission for local churches, he says, is not about inviting friends to church events, but "making common cause with the issues that people really care about in the world". "In my experience churches which are flourishing are those who are doing things in and for their community which resonate with the longings, needs and questions of the community, and out of that relationships grow which lead people on a journey.

"The common features of churches that are growing, both evangelical and catholic, are 1) They are serving their community, and 2) There is what I would call a place of nurture somewhere in the church – such as courses and events – where those who want to – and who do not feel pressurised to – can find out more about the faith.

"The catholic tradition of beauty in worship and engagement with the arts also resonates with our culture. In Britain the churches that are consistently growing are the cathedrals. One of the reasons is that that they have the resources to put on a style of worship that is astonishingly beautiful and draws people for whom beautiful music and liturgy feed their spirit."

His advice to clergy would also be not to be afraid to challenge people to make a serious commitment and go deeper in their discipleship. "That's why I became a priest. When I was in my early 20s I talked to my parish priest about my confusion about whether I might have a vocation and he challenged me hard to put it to the test by working in a hospice in South London, where he had contacts.

"That same day I packed up my job and started as a Ward Orderly in the hospice the following Monday. In some ways I think I learned everything there about ministry, and most importantly learned that God was present in the dying, and that death was not the tragedy our culture teaches us.

"I witnessed many miracles in that year – of people being reconciled to themselves and to God, and being released into death, rather than being restored to life. Death was the healing; healing arrived at the point when a person could say 'Father, into your hands I place my spirit.'"

"It was a liberating and transformative experience from which I went on to study for the priesthood."

....

Bishop Cottrell's books include From the Abundance of the Heart: Catholic Evangelism for all Christians *(Darton Longman and Todd) and* Hit the Ground Kneeling: Seeing leadership differently *(Church House Publishing). He has also co-written* The Pilgrim Course *– an introduction to Christianity for both seekers and those who are already Christian (see www.pilgrimcourse.org)*

Staying close to Jesus calls for a radical generosity to the poor

Steve Bradbury lectures in transformational development at Eastern College Australia. He spoke to Roland Ashby when he was director of the Christian overseas aid and development agency TEAR Australia, about his book, *Ordinary People, Extraordinary Love*, a moving and provocative account of his work with the poor of the two-thirds world. The interview appeared in the March 2002 edition of *TMA*.

RA: *Ordinary people, extraordinary love* is a disturbing and radical challenge to comfortable middle class Christians to put the poor at the centre of their Christianity. You are critical of the 'sweet sentimentality' of much communal worship, and compassion which is 'sweet and syrupy.' Why should caring for the poor, to quote C.B. Samuel, be 'part of the Christian's job description?'

SB: In his book *God of the Poor* Dewi Hughes says "it is impossible to really know Jesus and be indifferent to the plight of the poor." What I think he is encapsulating here is the idea that to be in relationship with Christ is to take the words and actions of Jesus seriously, and that inevitably leads us into engagement with the poor because they were such a focus of Jesus' attention.

As you explore both Old and New Testament teaching, you come across a huge abundance of material that reveals to us that God is a God of justice and compassion. Therefore we must be a people of justice and compassion.

Some go so far as to say that God has a bias for the poor, but I don't think that is true. God loves the poor and the rich equally, but because he loves us equally he has to take affirmative action on behalf of the poor who are weak because of their poverty.

RA: Do any particular Scriptures stand out for you?

SB: There are so many. One of the most disturbing passages in all of Scripture is Matthew Ch. 23 where we find Jesus hitting the Pharisees very hard. They were people who took the scriptures very seriously, so as someone who takes the scriptures very seriously I see Jesus very much speaking to people like me in that passage.

In verse 23 Jesus takes up the words of the prophet Micah (6:8) and says to the Pharisees 'you tithe your mint, your dill and your cummin, but you neglect the weightier matters of the law – justice, mercy and faithfulness.' Now what Micah was seeking to address was a people of God who had gone sadly astray. They were still heavily into worship in the sense of the ritual and the liturgy, but they failed to recognise that the true meaning of worship is service – service to God and service to a neighbour in need. Is this true of us as well? I think it often is. A close examination of church budgets, the content of our worship activities, the words we sing, and so on, often reveals an obsession with comfort and our own well-being. This is feel-good church. In this we reflect the society around us.

RA: Jesus also told the rich young ruler to sell his possessions and follow him. How are we to apply this uncompromising message to our own lives?

SB: Jesus' teaching clearly shows us that to follow him means that we must be engaged with the poor. For the rich young ruler the instruction was as radical as it gets. Sell everything and give the money to the poor.

Jesus didn't require the same thing of Zacchaeus. He was allowed, as it were, to keep half of what he had. Jesus was delighted by Zacchaeus' decision to give half of what he had to the poor and repay four-fold those he had 'ripped off'.

But the principle is clear – being a serious follower of Christ should have a radical impact on our holding of possessions and our use of wealth. It forces us to recognise that we are not owners, but stewards, in terms of the Bible's teaching about creation. Every one of us has a responsibility to prayerfully consider what God is asking of us with respect to our possessions and our wealth. And it will mean a radical generosity that will impact on our capacity to hoard for ourselves. The detail of that is going to vary from individual to individual.

RA: Who are the poor?

SB: The poor are the approximately two billion people in the world whose average daily protein intake is less than the average daily protein intake of an Australian household pet cat. The poor are the approximately 1.3 billion people whose income is US$1, or less, a day. There is a lot of mythology about the poor, that they are poor because of their own fault. Somehow they are to blame. Many of those of us who are not poor believe that if we were in their position we would not stay poor – we would find a way of battling our way out of that poverty. That reveals a tragic misunderstanding of the processes that create and sustain poverty. It is not easy if you have been born and raised in a poor community to rise above that poverty. Some do it and they are the exceptions, but most people can't, and it is because of the forces that keep that community poor.

Overwhelmingly the Scriptures teach us that poverty is a result of oppression and exploitation by the powerful and rich.

RA: Who are the oppressors today?

SB: One critical source of oppression is international trade where the law of the jungle is alive and well. Rich and powerful countries protect their own producers and force poor countries to accept disadvantageous arrangements. The exploitation of labour remains very ugly in many places. Desperate people are forced to work for pitiful wages. Even in a city like Melbourne there are many people working in the textile industry, the so called outworkers, earning $4-5 an hour.

The Jubilee 2000 campaign, which TEAR kick-started in Australia, has highlighted another oppressor. The structure of international debt is resulting in the movement of vast amounts of money from the poor world into the rich world. But there are also internal forces of oppression in most countries, and the poor are exploited by local elites.

RA: Of the situations you have seen, what has angered you the most?

SB: I once visited a pastor in India who took me to see a community of leprosy sufferers. As in biblical times they were outcasts, horribly marginalised.

He told me how sometime earlier he had encouraged them to move to this place and cultivate a block of vacant waste land. The block had clearly never been cultivated before – it was covered in boulders and rocks. With the pastor's encouragement, and with little more than disfigured stumps for hands, they managed to clear the land, to hoe it, to plant and nurture the seeds, until the crop was ready for harvesting.

Only then did the local big land owner appear and claim the land as his. Until then he hadn't said a word – he'd just watched them do all the preparation and the planting and said nothing, until they were ready to reap the harvest. Then he came with a truck and a bunch of thugs, claimed the crop and took over the land. They were powerless to resist.

I see in that event an echo of what is described in the scriptures again and again about the rich stealing the assets of the poor. Proverbs 13:23 says "the field of the poor man may yield much food, but it is swept away through injustice." Job 24:1-12, Psalm 10, and many other passages provide vivid descriptions of this process.

This raises the fundamental issue of how interventionist we believe God is. Now I do believe God intervenes directly, unilaterally, and miraculously, but I don't think that is God's normal modus operandi. As I look at the scriptures and reflect on my own experiences, I see a God whose primary way of intervention, to do justice or mercy, is by acting through his people. God's people are called upon to be agents of peace, of reconciliation, of love, of compassion.

RA: In the midst of this great poverty and sadness you have also encountered some remarkable people, whose extraordinary love and grace have provided you with many precious moments. Who amongst those people stand out?

SB: Grace Kaiso is certainly one. When I first met Grace he was pastor of an Anglican church in the Kalerwe slum community, in Kampala, Uganda. The more I spend time with Grace the more I am impressed by his demonstration of what the Gospel is all about.

The last time I was with Grace we were walking around the slum community and looking at the changes to that community as a direct result of Grace's intervention.

The community now has a school for the poor that the church has established. It has a health centre, an AIDS counselling centre, and there is fresh water being piped into that community because Grace had badgered the local authorities until they provided that water. There is much more adequate drainage now, and there are toilets in place that hadn't been there before, again because of Grace's intervention.

I asked him, 'Why are you doing all this?' And he said to me, 'I had only been in this parish a short time when I discovered that a quarter of the babies I was baptising were dying before they reached the age of six months. I had to ask myself what does it mean to be Jesus as a person in this place?'

It was this simple question which led to a dramatic shift in his ministry and resulted in a very positive response to the needs of the poor in that community.

The poor, the sick, the broken, were drawn to Jesus, and he was drawn to them. The reality is that if we want to stay close to Jesus we must walk where he walks. Grace really illustrates that for me.

RA: Talking about a broken people brings to mind the people of Afghanistan. Did you agree with the bombing?

SB: No I didn't. I have to say I am surprised at how quickly the Taliban were defeated by that bombing campaign, but I do not believe that bombing the daylights out of a poor country is the right way to protect the rich world from acts of terrorism.

As an American friend said to me just after the 11 September attacks, imagine if the world's and the US Government's response to the terrorist attacks of September 11 was to offer to the government of Afghanistan massive humanitarian aid – imagine what a message that would give to people living in situations of terrible poverty all around the world.

One cannot justify the acts of terrorism, but you have to recognise that those acts of terrorism have been nurtured by all manner of oppression and exploitation and manipulation by the great powers over many decades.

RA: How do you feel about Australia's treatment of asylum seekers?

SB: Deeply ashamed. There is no excuse for our harsh and compassionless treatment asylum seekers. The government is clearly compromised by the misinformation it has deliberately propagated, and in the critical pre-election period the Labor party failed to offer the kind of moral leadership we so desperately needed. The manipulative use of value-loaded language such as queue jumpers and illegal immigrants misrepresents the reality, and feeds Australian prejudices.

I understand that it is not appropriate to simply open our borders to anyone who wants to come here. But when people come unannounced and uninvited, indefinite incarceration in remote detention centres is neither reasonable nor humane. As for the so called Pacific Solution of funding detention centres in Nauru and PNG, the cost to the Australian taxpayer is going to be in excess of $500 million – a tragic case of economic irrationalism!

An activist for Gospel justice

Tim Costello AO, former CEO of World Vision Australia and now its Chief Advocate, talks to Roland Ashby about his book *Hope: Moments of Inspiration in a Challenging World*, a cornucopia of poignant reminiscences and candid, but ultimately hopeful, reflections. The interview appeared in the September 2012 edition of *TMA*.

RA: When I first saw the title of your book I remembered your moving accounts of the devastation and suffering you witnessed after the Asian tsunami disaster. My initial thought was how on earth have you held onto your faith, despite the apparent hopelessness of many of the situations you see?

TC: Curiously, the tsunami strengthened my faith, in an unexpected way. I discovered that faith and the resource of faith was all the people who were victims of the tsunami had to appeal to. And in Sri Lanka this is Muslim and Buddhist faith, not just Christian faith. One man said, "If I couldn't believe in God, I couldn't even get out of bed and even try again. I've lost my family, I've lost my home. That's all I've got."

So faith, I suddenly discovered, was a practical resource for human courage and hope. When we pose the question from the comparative safety of Australia, "Where is God at this distance from a tsunami?" we have the luxury of saying we're still protected and self-sufficient, and can ask the question in almost an objective way. Context determines the question, and their context was, without God, how can I start again?

RA: What do you say to those who simply cannot reconcile an all-loving and all-powerful God with such suffering?

TC: I don't think there is any intellectual or theological answer to theodicy (the problem of evil and suffering), other than, according to my understanding of faith, God has entered our suffering, taken death into himself in Jesus, embraced betrayal, unfair trial, torture, death, and profound injustice. I can only answer the question in a faith sense: that I believe God, who has shown us his face in Jesus, is no stranger to this.

RA: You believe in some way God enters our suffering and somehow transforms it.

TC: Absolutely.

RA: Even for those who suffered hideous deaths in the tsunami?

TC: Yes. I believe that because God has taken death into himself, that says for those who die unjustly, arbitrarily, quickly, that they are taken up into God, that death isn't the final word.

RA: There are some wonderfully hope-inspiring stories in the book. One particularly striking one is about 'The Circle of the Bereaved' – a group of Arabs and Jews in Jerusalem who have lost children in the Israel-Palestine conflict.

TC: I was so profoundly moved seeing Israeli Arabs and Israeli Jews sit and talk about the same loss. The common bond was grief; they had lost children. Arab parents had lost children to the Israeli defence forces, Jewish parents had lost children to the Shaheed suicide bombers. And they needed to see each other's faces, and to identify the grief and to, out of that, across the bonds of grief, ask what can we do together to stop the killing? That for me was one of the most hopeful things I've ever seen.

RA: One issue which agencies like yours are increasingly having to grapple with is climate change. What are you seeing as the effects of climate change in the areas that World Vision is working in?

TC: World Vision has 40,000 staff around the world, including scientists. What they see, simply, accords with what the climate scientists are saying. They will say, "For a millennium we always got two harvests, now we're getting only one. We always planted our seed at this time of year because that's when the birds arrive, now they arrive six weeks later. The season is shorter."

According to oral tradition going back 500-1000 years, they've never seen anything like this. I'm just back from Niger, Africa, where there are massive droughts. Now, the droughts that used to be once in every 15 years are once every two or three years. The experience resonates with what the scientists are saying, that we are warming, and that water and new arable land are being affected. Copenhagen was really the last attempt to find a global solution, but Copenhagen's problem, as we saw, and now in Rio is being made very clear, is that politicians who believe that climate change is real have this problem: they know any action now will not see effects until 2020 and beyond, and they're running for election in 2013 or 2014, and so the action now is costly without the pay off now.

That's why the world found it could not agree on acting, though they all believed they all needed to act, or all wanted someone else to be the first mover and act. That's a huge dilemma, not just for future generations, but for poor countries now which don't have the resources to respond.

RA: How are the Millennium Development goals progressing?

TC: We have been making significant progress in meeting the MDGs. We have nearly halved the number of people who are hungry and in absolute poverty, and we have also reduced the number of infant deaths by over 50 per cent.

There has been real global cohesion, but now, post the global financial crisis, things have fallen off because it's the developed world hurting, and so the developing world is way down the list of priorities for us. But the MDGs were really important. The great challenge now is what will the world agree to with the post 2015 new set of goals? That's what we're working on now.

RA: Archbishop Philip Freier has been calling for a renewed vision of the common good in Australia, and has suggested that the mining sector and the banks should share more of their wealth, for the betterment of all Australians. This relates to the Jewish concept of Shalom, which you talk about affectionately in the book.

TC: Shalom – which I sign all my letters with – is more than just a greeting of peace. Shalom is a word that means a right ordering in relationships, so let there be shalom in your marriages, in your business dealings, in your courts. It says don't let the judges sitting at the city gate weigh out grain with unfair weights, so the poor are disadvantaged. Shalom is saying that all of us live in a community where our own interests can never be pursued at the expense of others, and that the common good is profoundly important.

RA: In the book you also bemoan the lack of civility in public life.

TC: We are seeing it with toxic political rhetoric at the federal level, which I don't think you can just blame on a minority government; I think something has shifted there. Bob Katter talks of Ted Theodore and Curtin and Chifley, who lived in much worse times, who would never have made the sort of personal attacks that we see now.

In the Christian vision civility is fundamental to relationships. It is about seeing God in the other, and even if we disagree, showing respect, forbearance and constraint in our words.

RA: The book is very candid about the dangers of being a well known and popular public figure, and in the chapter *There is Violence in Me*, you write very honestly that the stronger the public light shines upon a person, the more intense the shadow. And you say it is the enemy within which has to be embraced.

TC: The first thing is to be aware of your shadow side. Most of us never see our shadow; we're looking ahead and it's the fact that it is unsighted which trips us up. For me, it is being aware that I much prefer success, I want the joys of the limelight; but the truth is, I have grown much more through my failures and mistakes, and as painful as they are, sometimes words spoken to me that make me angry but which are spoken in truth.

RA: People would not see you as a person of failure. What do you see as some of your failings?

TC: This will take the rest of your interview. I live very much in the present. I'm terrible at thinking ahead and organising, therefore thinking of others' birthdays, anniversaries, the things that really are matters of civility.

I think the march of what I'm doing is so important, everybody else must be on board, and I will get short tempered with people who haven't seen what I've seen and aren't bending their shoulder to the cause.

RA: You're a very busy activist Christian. What sustains your faith and activism?

TC: I have a prayer room in our house, where I write my diary each day. When I find it hard to pray, I write. I find it easier to pray actually when I'm jogging. When I'm moving, I get into a zone and find myself talking much more naturally to God and listening even more. I take seriously my devotional life, and try to read my Bible every day. And I keep up my worship attendance and on Sundays I'm often preaching.

RA: You talk about Bono, Martin Luther King and Catherine Hamlin with great affection in the book, and they have obviously been important sources of inspiration for you.

TC: I am very impressed with Bono who is grounded enough to say, "Celebrity is a nonsense. I've got it. I'm going to cash it in for good." That's why he's been such a champion of the poor and the making poverty history campaign.

Catherine Hamlin, who I call an Aussie saint, one of the early women at Sydney University to do medicine, could have had a fantastic career teaching surgery here, but chose to bury herself in Ethiopia with the most despised, women with fistula. And when you meet her, you feel that here is a person who has missed all the cynicism and shallowness of our culture because she has been so focused.

I named my youngest son after Martin Luther King. He was the first person who challenged me to say the Gospel isn't just for the private personal things; it's for the big issues – in his case racism, civil rights and the Vietnam War. And I, in this book, have tried to show how my faith relates to the big things.

RA: Perhaps surprisingly in the book you also admit to some admiration for George W. Bush.

TC: George W. Bush gave the largest increase in overseas aid, far greater than Clinton or Obama or others, and this is a story not known. The Pepfar [The President's Emergency Relief for AIDS Relief] Funds were a George Bush initiative.

RA: In the final chapter about your grandmother, you say she had some special advice for the family just before she died.

TC: She said, "Water them geraniums," which was puzzling because she didn't have any geraniums. It was only later we found the Henry Lawson story of that name about a woman battling. My grandmother was a fine Christian who was incredibly generous, who had her battles. And we realised she was passing on a message that it's those little things in life, unseen, unacknowledged, that are the measure of your faith.

Finding the Wright words to tell Bible truths

Dr Tom Wright, renowned New Testament scholar, Research Professor in New Testament and Early Christianity at St Andrew's University, Scotland, and former Bishop of Durham, talks to Roland Ashby about his faith and prayer life, his translation of the New Testament, why he finds Jesus' Divinity and Resurrection convincing, what heaven is, and how St Paul should be understood in relation to the Doctrines of Justification by Faith and the Penal Substitutionary Theory of the Atonement. Part I of the interview appeared in the August 2013 edition of *TMA*. Parts II and III of the interview follow in the next two chapters.

RA: You once said in an interview that you could never remember a time when you were not aware of the presence and love of God, and recalled an occasion when you were a young boy, perhaps six or seven, sitting by yourself and being completely overcome, coming to tears, by the fact that, "God loved me so much he died for me".

TW: Yes, that sense is still very important, very central. I have no idea what precipitated it. We were a very ordinary middle-of-the-road Anglican Church family. We were once-or-twice-every-Sunday people, but it was very unemotional. It was sort of old middle-to-low church but not evangelical, but we sang all the hymns and the readings were read.

RA: Could you give some idea of how the love and presence is manifested to you?

TW: It's curious because it's rather like in C.S. Lewis' *The Lion, the Witch and the Wardrobe*, which I was reading recently with great delight to one of my grandchildren, that when Lucy gets into the wardrobe thinking it's a wardrobe suddenly she's in Narnia. When she goes back to test it out with the other children it's just a wardrobe, and I think that's a very clear perception which Lewis had of how the presence of God works, that it will steal up on you when you're not expecting it.

Other times if you say, "Now I'm going to make some time and say my prayers," it may just be very cold and dry and nothing actually will 'happen'. However, if there is a wardrobe in the house we may just go on blundering into it by accident and sometimes we discover something more. Of course the old 16th and 17th century thing is still true about, as the old Scots theologians used to say, "Attending on the means of grace". That if you want to have a sense of the presence and love of God it will probably help if you go to church and join in public worship, go to the Eucharist, read scripture, say your prayers, and if you consciously think about being good and generous to the poor. In the Gospel Jesus says, "You'll recognise me in the faces of the poor that you help, or at least you may not recognise me but that's where you will actually be meeting me".

Do not assume anything will be automatic, but if life is framed in that way then 'stuff' will happen and you will come upon occasions when you will say, like Jacob, "Surely the Lord is in this place and I didn't know it".

I found as a pastor, again and again, that by praying at the beginning of the day, both for the people I knew I was going to meet and for the people I didn't know I was going to meet, that you can be confident that you'll get roughly the wisdom that you may need – probably not as much as they need, but you do the best you can.

In the psalms God says, "Seek my face," and we say, "Your face Lord will I seek, don't hide your face from me," and there's a sort of game of hide and seek going on: "Yes, I want to look for you. Please don't run away and hide because I was just getting there," and it seems to me that's a very true perception within Judaism and Christianity of how it is, it's elusive and yet not far away; tantalising.

RA: What is your daily prayer practice?

TW: I'm very old fashioned and have actually gone back to the 1662 Anglican prayer book. I use the Morning and Evening Prayer Service and extend the readings so that as well as a Psalm I usually have two bits of the Old Testament, one from the Torah, the first five books, and one from the rest of the Old Testament, and then likewise for the New Testament, I always have a reading from one of the Gospels and a reading, working through a cycle, from the rest of the New Testament as well.

I also love the great Canticles – the *Te Deum*, *Benedictus*, the *Magnificat* and the *Nunc Dimittis*. I sang them as a child and they're deeply inside me.

Because of my scholarship I also spend many hours of the week with the Bible texts open and 'doing business' with them.

RA: So you're really doing Lectio Divina, you're really living with them, inhabiting them?

TW: Yes. There's a fluidity between working out a particular problem exegetically and mulling over how a bit of scripture actually works, and pausing and praying about it, and applying it to my own life. This fusion makes it very exciting and dramatic for me.

When I was Bishop of Durham we used Lectio Divina for our staff meetings. After reading a scripture portion we would ask, "What is the one word that summarises for you what you're hearing out of this?" After listening to the responses, we would pause for a few minutes of silence, read the passage again, listen to more responses, and after about 20 minutes of this a discussion would emerge. The marvellous thing about that, again and again, was that during the rest of the day – and often our staff meetings would go on for about eight hours with a break for lunch – the things we had been mulling over in the morning would infuse the things we were talking about – even if it was nuts and bolts and you know, keeping the roof on this parish church or whatever – we would be holding it within the sense of the scripture that we had been inhabiting in the morning. It was a wonderful thing and we all enjoyed it.

RA: In 2011 you completed a new translation of the New Testament. I'm particularly interested in how this experience has deepened your faith.

TW: It certainly deepened my understanding because there is nothing like having to find solid English equivalents for forcing you to think deeper into what is actually going on. I was determined not to use the old 16th century words where I could avoid them because the New Testament in its original form is very lively. It's written in exciting street-level Greek, it's not highfalutin' classical, sonorous periods. There is a problem with the King James Version, from that point of view because the King James Version really is highfalutin' language with Latinate periods.

RA: Could you give some examples among the words of Jesus where the Greek is so much stronger than in any English translation.

TW: Yes. One example is when Mary and Jesus are in conversation in John 2 at the wedding of Cana. When Mary tells her son that the wine has run out Jesus' response in the Greek is very idiomatic, with almost a suggestion of

"Why are you bothering me with that?" So what I put in English was, "'Oh mother,' replied Jesus, 'what's that got to do with you and me?' " 'Mother' is a polite form of address but there's a slight exasperation in the tone, and I was trying to suggest something like, "Oh mother, do we have to?" I think there is a lot in the Gospels which actually does have a kind of quirky humour to it, a sort of typically Jewish humour, and I tried sometimes to bring that out.

Another example would be, "Render unto Caesar the things that are Caesar's and to God the things that are God's". That's the normal King James type translation. What I put is " 'Well then', said Jesus, 'you had better give Caesar back what belongs to Caesar, and – give God what belongs to God.' " But what I really wanted to put was, "You had better pay Caesar back in his own coin, hadn't you?" with its 'double entendre'.

RA: I notice that in the walking on the water story you translate Jesus as "It's me. Don't be afraid," whereas some prefer to see the Greek *egō eimi* as more than a simple identification - 'It's me'. Can the Greek be understood as 'I am' with an echo of Exodus 3:14, "I am what I am"?

TW: The question of the possible echo of Exodus is important, but the trouble is that the Greek there is perfectly idiomatic. *Egō eimi* can be translated 'It's me' but it also might have that Exodus resonance, but I decided to stick with how it would sound in idiomatic English. You know, maybe you could translate the divine name in Exodus 3 as 'It's me'?... and then maybe not.

RA: When Jesus is described as having 'compassion' or 'pity', these words are really quite tame compared with the Greek, aren't they?

TW: In Greek the word is *splangcha*, which is very vivid. It means "He felt it in his guts". The King James Version translates it as "He felt it in his bowels". The Greek actually is a very sort of physical earthy language in a way which English has got a bit prissy about.

RA: In the story of Jesus and the rich young man (Mark 10), I notice your version of 10v21 is 'Jesus looked hard at him, and loved him,' whereas the NIV leaves out 'hard'.

TW: The Greek there means something like "He looked into him," implying something like "Jesus stared deep into his eyes."

RA: Something like "looked into his soul"?

TW: Yes, that's the sort of implication.

RA: That's where the English really falls down sometimes isn't it, because it misses those really quite significant nuances. There are also examples where the English translation actually tends to obscure the true meaning. I notice, for example, that your translation says 'turn back and believe the good news' instead of the NIV's 'repent and believe the good news' in Mark 1:15. 'Repent' obviously has quite different overtones.

TW: Yes. That comes straight out of a rather startling experience I had many years ago reading Josephus's autobiography. Josephus was a late first century Jew who was a young general in the war against Rome and then changed sides and decided that God was on the side of the Romans and so he better be too.

Josephus describes a time in the mid-sixties of the first century when he is a young aristocratic general, and went north from Jerusalem to Galilee to confront the leader of one of the rebel groups and to tell him to give up his way of addressing the situation and to trust him, Josephus, for his. What Josephus says is, "Repent and believe in me," but that doesn't mean repent as in have a religious experience, it means, "Give up the way you're going, you're heading in the wrong direction mate, you had better stop that, turn around and come this way instead, and trust me for my agenda."

I remember sitting there thinking, "Josephus is writing about an incident in the mid-sixties, and that's what that phrase meant in the mid-sixties," which is roughly when Mark was written. So, undoubtedly we want to say, with hindsight, that there was a much fuller meaning hovering around, but for Jesus' first hearers I think it means, "You're going about the whole thing the wrong way. Stop doing that, trust me, I've got a better idea." I don't see this as being an either/or, this is not a de-mythologised reading at all because I think the whole message of Jesus is a God message addressed precisely into that situation.

RA: Are any words not translatable into English?

TW: Yes – the word *pistis*, for example. We usually translate it as 'faith' but it means loyalty, fidelity, trustworthiness, faithfulness. So, if one says 'faith' one thinks of a particular modern western construct to do with religion. But for them, it would have all of those other meanings of loyalty and trustworthiness built in.

RA: Jesus spoke Aramaic most of the time, so to what extent is it possible that much of the Greek translation is not always an accurate representation of what he said?

TW: Yes, this is a well-known puzzle, and my predecessor, but three, in the chair I currently sit in in Saint Andrews, Matthew Black, pioneered this in the fifties and sixties, translating the Greek back into Aramaic and then saying, "Isn't that interesting. Here we have, for instance, Matthew saying one thing, and Mark saying something slightly different. Both of them may be translations of the same Aramaic expression, or Mark, or one of them, may be saying something which might well be a slightly misunderstood way of expressing an Aramaism.

This is difficult for one reason in particular, that we have very little first century Palestinian Aramaic. Apart from some bits in the Old Testament and the Dead Sea Scrolls we don't have very much relevant Aramaic at all, so it's tricky to reconstruct the language. The other thing is, of course, that though I'm sure Jesus' first language was Aramaic, all that we know about the way that human cultures work is that many, many peoples over historical periods have had at least three languages and I think it's highly likely that Jesus and his first followers were at least fluent in street-level Greek; they might not have been able to read Homer, but they could get by. I have no difficulty in thinking that Jesus and Pilate had a long conversation in Greek. It's like English in parts of Africa or India, basically it's everybody's second language.

RA: How many of the sayings attributed to Jesus actually belong to him, do you believe, given that the well-known Jesus seminar scholars have suggested that many do not?

TW: Yes. I have very little trouble with any of the sayings as they stand. There are some where I think you can see that they have been really cleverly shaped by the Evangelists, but in my book *Jesus and the Victory of God* I mount a historical argument for how we can understand Jesus in his context, and it's quite remarkable. I mean I've spent a lot of my life studying Second Temple Judaism, and actually when you understand how the Jewish world of the first century works, all sorts of sayings which previously seemed to be a bit tricky, about which you might ask, "Why would Jesus say that?" have a very subtle different meaning which fits in perfectly, like a hand into a glove, in that context. So by the historical reconstruction of the entire period I have found again and again – and I'm not the only one to do this – that the sayings come up in three dimensions, and you think, "Oh my goodness, he actually could have said that."

But yes, of course there is a tradition in historiography going right back to Thucydides, that writers will not necessarily give you the actual words, but they will construct a speech which is probably shorter than what was originally given because people spoke at length. When Paul spoke in Athens before the Areopagus he did not just speak for two and a half minutes, but the speech in Acts 17 you could read out in two and a half minutes. So, we have to conclude that Luke has put it together and scrunched it down to its bare minimum. If he's done that with Paul I think it's quite likely he was doing that with Jesus as well.

God came back, in Jesus, to take charge

Dr Tom Wright, renowned New Testament scholar, Research Professor in New Testament and Early Christianity at St Andrew's University, Scotland, and former Bishop of Durham, talks to Roland Ashby. In Part I he reflected on his faith and prayer life and his translation of the New Testament. In Part II, which appeared in the September 2013 edition of *TMA*, he explains why he finds Jesus' Divinity and Resurrection convincing. Part III of the interview, which considers St Paul's theology, follows in the next chapter.

RA: Which Gospel passages for you are the most powerful in convincing you of the truth of Jesus' divinity? Liberal theologian Marcus Borg, in *The Meaning of Jesus: Two Visions* – in which you dialogue with him – describes Jesus as a "mystic, healer, wisdom teacher, social prophet, a movement initiator". So why do you think he's more than those things?

TW: I would want to say very clearly that I think Marcus Borg is absolutely right that Jesus is all those things; but I think he was much more.

The problem with discussing the divinity of Jesus is that the modern western perception of divinity as applied to Jesus usually assumes that we know what divinity is, and then tries to pin that on Jesus. I think we have to turn it around and re-express it in first century terms. Often, I find, today's would-be orthodox Christians are actually in danger of Docetism, of having a sort of divine Jesus who only seems to be human but isn't really.

The critical matrix for all this in the world of the first century is that Jesus lived in a world where people were waiting for God to come back. So, the issue is not, 'Here is this man who is so extraordinary, we find ourselves having to tell God-stories about him'. The issue is rather, 'Something has happened here which has made us conclude that God has come back and has done the drastic thing he always promised,' and so we find ourselves having to tell Jesus-stories about God; I think the New Testament is coming at it that way.

So rather than proving the divinity of Jesus, it is, if you like, proving the Jesusness of God, of Israel's God. Again, our difficulty here is that the word 'God' is usually heard in the western world as a deist God or an Epicurean God, a kind of absentee landlord who is up in the sky somewhere, and Israel's God was never really like that.

The first place that alerted me to this was Luke 19 where Jesus is coming to Jerusalem riding in on the donkey and telling this story about a king who goes away and comes back. Now many people in the church have assumed that that is a story about Jesus himself going away and coming back in the second coming, but as I and others have argued – and this is not my pet theory, it's something many people have said – the story doesn't really work very well like that, and actually the whole point of Luke 19 is that your enemies are going to come and destroy the city because you did not know the day of your visitation, and in the Greek it is clearly divine visitation that is meant. In other words, Israel's God went away, left you with tasks to do, and this is what it looks like when he comes back. Now that's a very different way of talking about the divinity of Jesus from how most people have done it, but I think it's actually the way the New Testament itself is encouraging us to do it, and I find massive backup for that in Paul, John, Hebrews and Revelation.

RA: You have said that Jesus was Yahweh returned, a new Temple, in which heaven and earth came together.

TW: In my recent book *How God became King*, I say that the divinity of Jesus is the key in which the music is set but it isn't the tune that is being played. The tune that is being played is not simply, 'Jesus is God. Oh wow, isn't that extraordinary,' but this Jesus in whom the living God is coming back is setting up his kingdom, which means something political and social, as well as what we think of as religious. The returning God is coming back to be King, and while his kingship is redefined around the servant ministry of the cross, it's still a case of 'He's come back to take charge'; that's what it's all about.

RA: You have said that the cross was also the place where heaven and earth paradoxically meet.

TW: Yes. I think this comes very clearly in John but I think it is there in the other evangelists as well. With John, of course, so much of the Gospel is about the coming together of heaven and earth. It begins with the Genesis scene which is about God creating heaven and earth; so as soon as it says, 'In the beginning,' there is a resonance with Genesis 1. Then what happens is that the 'Word' became flesh and dwelt in our midst, and the Greek word for 'dwell' means 'pitched his tent or tabernacle'; in other words this is a Temple thing, and the point of the Temple is that's where heaven and earth were supposed to come together. So, John is telling us up front: in Jesus we have the new Temple, the new place where heaven and earth come together.

RA: Why do you find the reports of Jesus' resurrection appearances convincing?

TW: I address this question in my 700-page book *The Resurrection of the Son of God*. Resurrection was a big 'no, no' in the Greco-Roman world, and if it's ever mentioned it's sneered at: 'We all know that doesn't happen, don't be so silly.' So we have to ask, 'Why did belief in resurrection arise and why was it so sharply defined?' because even in Pharisaic Judaism, where resurrection had been what they believed, it wasn't that sharply defined.

If the stories about the resurrection had been made up they wouldn't have looked like what we have. They are much more likely to have had the risen Jesus shining like a star in the sky, as in Daniel 12. However, the risen Jesus doesn't shine, nor are the stories of the resurrection interlaced with scriptural reference, which is very interesting because the stories of the crucifixion are interlaced with scriptural reference, such as Psalm 22 and Isaiah 53. So if somebody was writing the story of the resurrection later, at the time the Gospels were written, in the 60s or 70s of the first century – it would be extraordinary to think that they would take out all the echoes of scripture. It's much easier to say that the stories of resurrection are put into the Gospels as a result of vivid eye witness, stories that would have been repeated again and again.

There are about 25 other points, but this is the only other point I will give you today: the place of the women in the story, and Mary Magdalene in particular. If somebody had made up the story of the resurrection, even 10 years later, let alone 30 years later, they sure as anything would not have the women as witnesses, or if they did these would be unimpeachable, impeccable women of known high quality and reliability, not somebody from whom seven demons had been cast out, because there was a sort of crazy counterintuitive belief about the place of the women.

Even in 1 Corinthians 15:4-8, when Paul gives us the official Church version – 'He was buried, raised on the third day... appeared to Peter... to James, then to all the apostles, and last of all he appeared to me' – where are the women? They've gone. Why? Because this is the public tradition that the Church had now developed, and they were obviously nervous about the women; but the Gospels keep them in because that's where they really were.

I grew up in a world where most theologians were saying, 'Of course nobody believes in the resurrection today. It's just a myth, a metaphor.' Well okay, explain the rise of Christianity then! It's jolly well not easy to do.

RA: This brings us back to Marcus Borg. In *The Meaning of Jesus: Two Visions* he says that, "The truth of the Easter stories and of Easter itself does not depend on their being literally and historically factual." He adds, "There's no doubt that the followers of Jesus continued to experience Jesus as a living reality after his death, but this was more an experience of his spirit, including through visions, apparitions, mystical experiences and the sense of his presence." How does your understanding of Jesus' resurrection appearances differ from this?

TW: The Greek word for resurrection is *anastasis*, which means 'a standing up'. That word simply didn't mean what is meant by, 'John Brown's body lies a-mouldering in the grave and his soul goes marching on'; it was always about bodies, and hence the *anastasis*, the standing up. It's not a word about a continuing spiritual experience of somebody else.

In AD 70 Titus destroyed the Temple and brought thousands of Jewish prisoners back to Rome in triumph, including Simon bar Giora, who was supposedly the King of the Jews at the time. He was dragged along at the back of the procession and then executed in the prison under Capital Hill in Rome.

Supposing a few days after that one or two of his shattered followers got together, but one of them says, 'I think he's been raised from the dead,' and another asks him, 'What do you mean, he's been raised from the dead?' and he replies, "I have a sense of his presence with me, I can feel him around. I think he's somehow still with us and wants us to carry on with his work.' What they would say to him, as good Second Temple Jews is, 'Wow, you may be right. Maybe he sort of is with us, but why did you say he's been raised from the dead?' because these are two very different things. These meanings are not fluid, they're very precise. If Marcus wants to go the route he does then the big historical explanation he has to give is why so early, as early as Paul himself, people would actually use language to describe that ongoing spiritual experience which always and everywhere up to that point referred to an actual event in which somebody who had been physically dead was physically alive again. That's the challenge.

St Paul's theology often misunderstood

Dr Tom Wright, renowned New Testament scholar, Research Professor in New Testament and Early Christianity at St Andrew's University, Scotland, and former Bishop of Durham, talks to Roland Ashby. In the third and final part of the interview, which appeared in the October 2013 edition of *TMA*, he reflects on St Paul's theology, justice and beauty, and the nature of heaven.

RA: You have said that Paul's words in relation to the penal substitutionary theory of the atonement have been misunderstood by many.

TW: Paul's big picture – what he is really all about – is a ministry of reconciliation.

For Paul the ministry of reconciliation is through the death of Jesus. In 2 Corinthians 5 he says: "God was in the Messiah reconciling the world to himself, not counting their trespasses against them, and then entrusting us with the message of reconciliation," and then he says, "For our sake God made him to be sin who knew no sin, so that in him we might become the righteousness of God." 2 Corinthians 5:21 is a controversial verse, but it is about Jesus as being the place where, and the means by which, God has dealt with sin.

But then we find in Romans 8:3-4 Paul saying that God condemned sin in the flesh of the Son, which is a very subtle thing. He condemns sin, which is, in a sense, penal, and the passage begins, "There is therefore now no condemnation for those who are in Christ Jesus because… God condemned sin," so the fact that there is no condemnation for us is dependent on the condemnation which was issued in the flesh of Jesus, so it is both penal and substitutionary.

But it's interesting that Paul doesn't say God condemned Jesus; he says, "God condemned sin in the flesh of Jesus". The danger with the doctrine of penal substitution is when people say, as they often do, that God basically punished Jesus. It's a very, very important doctrine but it's regularly misunderstood and only when we put it in its proper biblical context will it do, because otherwise this is not reconciliation, otherwise this is some odd, almost commercial, transaction, and that's not reconciliation. So, whatever Paul says about penal substitution it must serve the notion of the ministry of reconciliation.

RA: You have also said that we can't be justified by simply believing in justification by faith, and often it seems that people make that mistake. You have explained justification by faith beautifully by analogy with a person with whom we are truly in love, and the person loves us unconditionally, not because of what we do.

TW: We still have the Puritan streak in many parts of the Church today, where people will say, "Unless you believe justification by faith your salvation is in question". The analogy about love illustrates how justification by faith works, that if somebody only gives you and shows you love when you've done certain things, as it were to earn it, then that's not actually love at all, that's some kind of a contractual relationship. Part of the danger with justification by faith is that in some theological theories it almost turns into a contract. But that's not faith because that's not love, and faith is the sort of extraordinary glad-eyed astonishment at realising that there's this wave of love coming at you, regardless of whether you have merited it.

RA: You have also said that faith is a gift of God through the spirit, and no one can say Jesus is Lord unless by the spirit, and we're called to be the faithful people of God through the spirit. Why do you think the gift seems to be given to some and not to others? What about those who cannot accept faith but live good, loving and compassionate lives? You have said that the spirit is at work in all sorts of ways, and we don't always have to get the theory right.

TW: The question you've asked is the one which, I think, the whole New Testament leaves us with. I was quoting Paul obviously, 1 Corinthians 12, where he says no one can say Jesus is Lord except by the spirit, and then Ephesians 2, where he says, "By grace you have been saved through faith and that's not of yourselves, it's the gift of God". This is a way of making sure that when somebody believes, there is no sense that they are, as it were, standing tall and saying, "I'm going to pin my flag on God's map and God will like that". No, it's not like that at all. It's all coming at us from God's side.

And then, as you imply, we're left with two choices: one being that you become a Universalist and believe God simply loves everyone, saves everyone, and faith is simply that some people happen to recognise that this is happening while others don't. I find that very difficult to square with the New Testament and with Jesus or Paul, Peter or Revelation. It seems to me that what happens to people in their lives here actually does have long-term consequences, even though that's hard to plot, and as with much of this, we're out in the area of mystery and nobody quite knows.

But the Old Testament does have a theology of election, as in the election of Israel, and there are hints that Christians are working with that and developing it, in relation to the Church, but they don't develop it very far. Paul says in I Thessalonians, "We know beloved ones that God has chosen you, because when we preach to you our Gospel came not only in word but in power and in the spirit and with full conviction". In other words, you can see that God was choosing you, but I don't think Paul necessarily means therefore nobody else in the marketplace that day was chosen by God, it means that you're the kind of pilot project, as it were. So, I think we there do get towards a mystery which the New Testament doesn't foreclose on, and I would rather take care not to try and push beyond where I think the text takes us.

RA: Several passages including 1 Corinthians 13 and Romans 8:38-39 suggest that Paul had experienced a profound, perhaps mystical, union with Christ. I note that Albert Schweitzer believed that "the centre of Paul" was what he called "Christ-Mysticism", something you say Pauline scholar E.P. Sanders agreed with.

TW: For me, the clearest and sharpest passage in relation to this is surely Galatians 2:19, where Paul says, "I am crucified with the Messiah. I am, however, alive – but it isn't me any longer, it's the Messiah who lives in me. And the life I do still live in the flesh, I live within the faithfulness of the Son of God, who loved me and gave himself for me." Those lines have a sense that they grow out of a kind of a passionate embrace; that Paul has been grasped by this love, and that when he looks at the cross he doesn't think first and foremost of a commercial transaction, he thinks of it as this incredible love to which he can do nothing other than respond with love and gratitude.

What did Paul mean when he talked about 'being in Christ'? I think he would say it is about coming to the point of knowing that one is grasped by Christ's love. For some it will be a head knowledge that gradually turns into heart knowledge, for others it will be an amazing heart knowledge which will then cause them to think afresh.

RA: You have also said that you see a connection between justice, beauty, music and the arts.

TW: It seems to me that in the New Testament we have constantly flitting before our eyes a vision of new creation, and the vision of new creation is a vision of the world put right, and that goes back to the Old Testament, to passages like Isaiah 11, or the Psalms; such as Psalms 96 and 98, often talking about the whole creation thrilled because God is sorting it all out.

Justice is a way of talking about things being put right, and unless we are being 'putting right' sort of people now, why should people believe us when we say that in Jesus, God has put things right and is putting things right?

Music and the arts remind us, that though the world is messy and awkward and has horror in it, there is also this thing called beauty which is actually what God's world is all about. Justice and beauty ultimately go together.

I grew up singing in church choirs, and for me it's hard to imagine faith without music. We forget that the great western music tradition comes out of the monasteries and then the renaissance, and actually if it hadn't been for the Christian tradition there is no good evidence that western classical music would have become what it became. People don't usually hear a Brahms symphony or a Wagner opera, and say, "Oh yes, that's all because of the Christian tradition," but actually if you track it back that's where it all comes from.

RA: You have said we've become increasingly left-brain dominated in the West. Why do you think this is a particular problem for people of faith?

TW: By and large the right brain does the big picture stuff: narratives, myths, metaphors, music, religion, faith; and the left brain does fiddly little details. For me as a scholar and person of faith the two obviously have to go together!

RA: What do you think of as heaven?

TW: In the Bible heaven is God's space, and part of the point of heaven from the very beginning is that God's space and our space are supposed to mesh together. In the Temple the Jews believed they did mesh together, and then the Rabbis believed that even if you weren't in the Temple or if it had been destroyed, when you sat down together and studied Scripture, then heaven and earth came together there.

I believe that that is still true. Jesus said, "Where two or three gather in my name I'm there in the midst." So heaven is a present reality and when John, in Revelation, says, "There was an open door in heaven etc," he's not seeing a vision of the future, he's seeing a vision of the present, the heavenly dimension of present reality.

Most people, when they say, "What do you think about heaven?" mean "What do you think about the ultimate future?" In *Surprised by Hope* I argue that in the New Testament the ultimate hope is not heaven, it is the new heavens and the new earth. The end of Revelation is not about saved souls going up from earth to heaven but about the new Jerusalem coming down from heaven to earth. So the old joke, which wasn't original to me but which I use frequently is: "heaven is important but it's not the end of the world."

The ultimate end is the new heavens and the new earth, so I want to say all we know about where God's people are after death is very simple. Paul says, in Philippians I, "My desire is to depart and be with Christ which is far better," but then we note that in Philippians 3 he says, "He will change our lowly body to be like his glorious body," and that's the resurrection. We're not told what it means to be with Christ in the time after death. The important point is the ultimate future and then the trust that in the intermediate period we will be with Christ which is far better.

When I took my father's funeral two years ago, I made sure that we were very affirming of a two-stage journey after death: That great hymn *For all the Saints* affirms this. The first, temporary stage is thus described: *The golden evening brightens in the west, soon, soon to the faithful warriors cometh rest. Sweet is the calm of paradise the blest, alleluia.* Then follows: *But lo, there breaks a yet more glorious day, the saints triumphant rise in bright array.* We have forgotten that it's a two-stage post-mortem story.

Understanding and Engaging with Islam

Violent world needs the 'Jihad' of Jesus

In the light of a global series of religiously motivated terrorist acts, Dave Andrews, writer and community worker for TEAR Australia, warns of the dangers of 'closed set religion'. He spoke to Roland Ashby about his book *The Jihad of Jesus – the Sacred Nonviolent Struggle for Justice*. The interview appeared in the December 2015 edition of *TMA*.

Dave Andrews experienced first-hand what happens when inter-religious tensions erupt into savage violence when he lived in India in the early '80s. Following the assassination of Indira Gandhi by her Sikh body guards in 1984, Hindus were slaughtering Sikhs in their thousands in retaliation.

"Hearing the screams of a terrified young Sikh family on the roof of their home which was being attacked by an angry Hindu mob intent on murder, I and some neighbours decided to try to prevent them from entering.

"Amidst the chaos and terror we stood at the door with our hands together pleading with them not to hurt the family. The mob screamed and yelled and came closer and we knew that if they had begun to hit us, then it would have ended in us being cut to pieces. But we looked into their eyes, we begged them, we prayed desperately, and they hesitated… before running off in search of others. Then the Army arrived and the mob fled."

This experience is one of the reasons, he explains, why he stands up for Muslims. "I know how quickly things can turn and how the mob mentality can take over; and how we can scapegoat people and end up slaughtering innocent people in the process."

This human capacity and potential for violence, he says, has made him confront his own dark side, and develop a spiritual practice which allows him to be centred and focused in the midst of turmoil.

The heart of this practice, he says, is his own version of the Jesus prayer: "Jesus, Saviour, may I know your love and make it known." "For me, the most important place for that prayer is in the nanosecond between action and reaction, where I try, rather than react and retaliate, to slow down, to create a space between action and reaction and in that place I critically reflect on myself and I pray that prayer."

He repeats it silently during his time of prayer and meditation each morning and evening. "But what's really important is that I learn it by heart and it becomes the prayer of my heart, and I can pray it without thinking, as a way of focusing and centring on the love of God revealed in Jesus.

"So entering that deeper place of love becomes the formative way of shaping the way I engage with the Muslim community and the conflict between Christians and Muslims. This is also to enter a place of humility, and of taking the log out of my own eye before I try to take the speck out of somebody else's."

In explaining the confrontational title of his book *The Jihad of Jesus*, he writes: "Jesus embodied the original Jihad of non-violent struggle for inspirational personal growth and transformational social change… [He] demonstrates a life of radical non-violent sacrificial compassion as the only way of life that can save us from destroying ourselves and our societies".

He believes understanding the term 'Jihad' is critical for Christian/Muslim dialogue. "My Muslim friends say that the extremists have co-opted the word 'Jihad' and used it as a by-word for terror in a way that's not true to the original understanding of Jihad in the Qur'anic text. They would say the words *Jihad* and *Jihada* are used 35 times in the Qur'an, and only four times is the word associated with violence. So they'd say the overwhelming emphasis of the idea of Jihad in the text itself affirms a non-violent struggle for justice.

"Where it is associated with violence, it is the sort of violence that in the West would be permitted according to the theory of Just War: if, in a struggle for justice you need to use force, you should never be the aggressor, it should only be defensive; then in the conflict you should make sure that you protect other people of other traditions and religions, never destroy their holy places or property. You have to guard against the death of any innocent civilians, never use force to coerce people into conversion and if there's any sign of a willingness to make peace, you make peace, even if you're sceptical about whether people mean it or not because peace is what Allah wants."

When interpreting the Bible or the Qur'an, Dave says context is crucial. "My Muslim friends would say even more than that; they would say if we are going to interpret the Qur'an fully and faithfully we need to recognise that every surah in the Qur'an except one begins with *Bismillahir-Rahman ir-Rahim* – in the name of God the most merciful and gracious and compassionate. And they say they wouldn't see that as an invocation that they set aside and then do their interpretation; they say we should see that as a hermeneutic for interpretation. So when we invoke the mercy and grace and compassion of God, that should then be the hermeneutic for interpreting the text and any interpretation of the text that does not reflect the mercy and grace and compassion of God is not of God. Now, to me, that is profound as a hermeneutical way of engaging the text and I think it makes all the difference."

In his encounter with the Samaritan woman at the well, he believes Jesus showed how to dialogue with people of other faiths.

"I believe that the relationship between Jesus and the Samaritans is analogous to the relationship between Christians and Muslims. I think what's really interesting in Jesus' conversation with the Samaritan woman is that, first of all, he acknowledges the contribution of the Jews; and I think both Christians and Muslims both need to honour the Jewish tradition that we both derive from.

"The second thing is that then he is really clear that he doesn't operate in the way that the disciples did in wanting to bring down fire on somebody else who is different.

"In the conversation the woman begins by pointing out that they've got very different traditions, but he doesn't enter into a debate about that, he just acknowledges it and he accepts that those distinctions are there. What he affirms in the relationship is the universality, and that the fundamental call is to worship God in spirit and truth, regardless of what your tradition is.

"Then they have a conversation about the Messiah and I think it's very intriguing that he actually, in the context of that conversation, affirms the importance of the Messiah in a way that she can relate to and can embrace, yet he doesn't expect her to change her religion from Samaritan to Jew. In my engagement with my Muslim friends, I want to affirm who Jesus is as the Messiah or *Masih* – something that's acknowledged by both the Qur'an and the Gospels. But I do not believe I am being called to convert Muslims to Christianity. I believe I am called as a follower of Jesus simply to witness to Jesus in what I say and do with my Muslim friends."

Jesus' dialogue with the woman is an example of "open set religion", he explains. "Jesus challenged religion as a closed set, which defines itself over against the other, is hard-hearted and has a closed mindset, with hard doctrinal differences competing with one another in a zero sum game.

"Jesus called people from different traditions to respond to the Spirit in an open set way, which is inherently non-violent."

Despite the brutal acts of violence around the world he remains positive about the future. "I am inspired by such Muslims as Muhammad Ashafa and Christians such as James Wuye.

"Muhammad Ashafa was brought up in Nigeria in a very strict, austere Islamic tradition where his family taught him that his role was to aspire to the return of an Islamic Caliphate, and he was very attracted to that. He found himself in conflict with a pastor by the name of James Wuye and they formed militias fighting against each other. They killed one another's families and in one of the conflicts, James Wuye's arm was chopped off. So serious violence. But both of them were converted – not to one another's religion – but to a God of mercy, grace and compassion. So open set rather than closed set. A God who was bigger than their religion, who encouraged them to reach out to one another. They forgave each other. They became friends. They established the Christian–Muslim Peace Centre and now they train teams of Pastors and Imams to go into conflict areas to negotiate peace."

Although Dave was raised as a Baptist, he began attending St Andrew's Anglican Church in South Brisbane after returning from India 30 years ago, and helped to establish a local network of residents called the Waiters' Union, offering friendship and assistance to the most disadvantaged and marginalised in the community – including Aborigines, refugees and people with disabilities.

"We called ourselves the Waiters' Union because we wanted to wait on God and wait on our neighbours. Our main focus is on developing friendships, rather than providing services. We invite people into our homes and visit them in their homes. We picnic and barbeque together. We run support groups for people going through a crisis. We help settle refugees. We advocate for the marginalised.

"We see ourselves as a catalyst for transformation seeking to create community which reflects the radical compassion of God."

....

The Jihad of Jesus – The Sacred Nonviolent Struggle for Justice
is published by Wipf and Stock.

Understanding and Engaging with Islam

Battle for the soul of Islam underway

How are we to understand Islamic terrorism? An expert in Muslim–Christian relations, Dr John Azumah, speaks to Roland Ashby. This interview with the Associate Professor of World Christianity and Islam at Columbia Theological Seminary, who was born in Ghana into a Muslim family, appeared in the February 2015 edition of *TMA*.

RA: In a recent article you argue that just as it would be wrong to judge Christianity on the behaviour of some Christian extremist groups, such as the Lord's Resistance Army in Uganda which quotes the Bible, it would be wrong to judge Islam on the violent behaviour of extremists.

JA: Yes, even though they claim to be Muslims, and they are doing this in the name of Islam as they see it, they are not playing according to the rules of the game, and the nature of their attacks is a fundamental area where they are departing from the vast majority of Muslims. First, no one has the right to just get up and declare Jihad. You've got to have the right qualifications and authority to do that.

Jihad is a theory of war very similar to the Christian theory of Just War and for a long time in history Muslims and Christians were not any different in their theories of war and their use of violence to extend their frontiers or their influence. There are very clear regulations about the conditions under which Jihad can be declared and conducted. But these groups are not following the laid-out regulations. Targeting and attacking civilians, women and places of economic interest is a clear violation of the regulations of Jihad.

RA: On what grounds could it be argued that Islam is a religion of peace?

JA: There are 1.6 billion Muslims in the world today. Now, if Islam was a violent religion, we have 1.6 billion potential suicide bombers, and yet we know that is simply not the case. We know the vast majority of Muslims read the same Qur'an, they recite the same prayers daily and yet they are just going about their ordinary lives, they are concerned about things that you and I are concerned about, their children's education, jobs, health issues; they are just ordinary people and yet they hold very dearly to this religion also.

We should also remember the Muslim groups who are risking their lives and fighting such terrorists and have been killed protecting vulnerable minorities.

I come from a context where I lived with Muslims, and I have Muslim relations in my family, and they don't recognise this violent face of Islam as part of their religion.

Of course it is true that while some verses in the Qur'an speak about peace in regard to the relations with people of other religions, there are a lot of verses that also talk about violence – and we cannot run away from that. The Qur'an can sometimes be very schizophrenic. It has some wild mood swings. It says very positive, very compassionate things in one breath; in the next breath it says very contemptuous, very belligerent things. Therefore Muslim groups, depending on where they are, their social-political context, and their own individual personalities and psychological makeup, tend to gravitate towards one or the other face of the Qur'an.

But it comes down to interpretation. In regard to the Qur'an there are two main keys of interpretation: one is called the principle of abrogation and the other is called the principle of context of revelation.

The principle of abrogation says that where there are two conflicting texts the later text abrogates – cancels out – the earlier text. And so if there's a verse, for instance, that says 'take Christians as your friends' – and there is a verse like that – and another, later verse, which says 'don't take Christians as your friends' – and there is a verse like that too – this later one is the one that has more authority.

The other way of interpretation is to apply the principle of 'context of revelation', in which people ask themselves under what context and circumstances was this text revealed. They look at the specific context, time and group of people. Moderate Muslims will insist on considering the context of revelation when interpreting the Qur'an.

The principle of abrogation came to be enshrined at a time that Islam was an empire, Islam was dominant. Islam never saw itself becoming a minority religion, let's say in Australia, and so in that kind of empire mindset interpreters said things that they never foresaw would be problematic.

Moderate Muslims believe you can't apply a seventh century text literally, and they prefer historical criticism, and become speculative and philosophical in the way they look at the text.

The fundamentalist groups tend to be very literalist and, therefore, if you read the Qur'an literally, like the Old Testament, you have mega problems. Unfortunately there are Christians who are just as 'Biblicist' as the fundamentalist Muslims. The Bible says this, period. So in regards to interpreting the Qur'an, the fundamentalists are the Biblicists, if you like, of Islam; they take the text very literally.

Part of the problem that Islam is having to deal with – the two faces of Islam – is embedded in Muhammad's ministry or mission. In his Mecca period, which lasted from 610 to 622, he was a peaceful preacher. He encouraged his believers to be steadfast, tolerant, not to fight back, and would just warn people about the consequences of rejecting God's word. Then in the later Medina phase, when he became a ruler, the Commander-in-Chief, a legislator, the revelations there assumed much more belligerent, militaristic and political undertones.

So you have these two faces of Muhammad's mission; and the principle of abrogation simplistically put says that Medina abrogates Mecca and therefore the Medina becomes mainstream. However, the context matters and those who argue for the importance of context say that the Medina face of Islam took shape in the context of having to deal with aggression from Mecca. Indeed, some major Muslim scholars have argued for the reversal of the abrogation – that Mecca should abrogate Medina.

RA: You have also said that the battle for the soul of Islam is earnestly underway.

JA: Yes, and I can only see that battle intensifying because there was a time that the moderate progressive liberal voices in Islam tended to be very stunted and very small. Now there is a growing swell of momentum because these moderates are tired and fed-up, and there's a sense of defiance now.

They believe they now have to speak up regardless of the consequences and they are saying that these radical groups are hijacking their religion. They don't want to have anything to do with this violence and hatred in the name of their religion, in the name of their Prophet, in the name of their God. They refuse that and they want to reclaim Islam back for what they think it should be.

So you have a lot of Muslim scholars now who are genuinely putting their lives on the line, coming out to challenge the extremists because they see this as a battle not just on the battlefield, but an ideological battle for the hearts and minds of people.

And we should not forget that Muslims are the overwhelming victims of the violence. Ninety-five per cent of the victims of Muslim militant violence are Muslims themselves and so Muslims see this as an existential threat to themselves, more than to you and I.

This is not going to be a battle that can be won in the university campuses, in Harvard or Oxford or Melbourne. This battle can only be won in the Madrasa, in the Qur'an schools, and what Muslims teach their young children. It is not what Muslims tell you and I that matters; it is what Muslims tell themselves and what Muslims tell their young people. That is what is going to be crucial in this battle that is going on.

RA: You have said that Islam is not the problem, but it has a problem, and part of this problem is Dhimmitude, and the attitude to women.

JA: Yes, when it comes to Dhimmitude, that is where I think Islam has a major problem. This is the teaching that if you are a non-Muslim in an Islamic State, you are a second-class citizen. It tends to feed the spiritual narcissism in Islam that Muslims are the purest and the 'best community'; all others are not only impure and inferior but they can also be disposed of, and that is a very dangerous teaching. But there are Muslim scholars who are engaging with this and who argue for equal citizenship for all citizens. A leading progressive voice on this was a former President of Indonesia, Abdurrahman Wahid. He said he did not subscribe to Dhimmitude and preferred the Indonesian constitution which gives equal citizenship to all people.

With women, there is also a serious problem. There are a lot of texts in the Qur'an that talk about women as second-class, and who are subservient to men. Now, again, Muslim women have been challenging this and some of the progressive Muslim men are challenging this and they are saying, look, it's not just about the rights of minorities, it is also about the rights of women.

RA: What are the conditions which lead to terrorism and to what extent do you believe that the West is responsible for Islamic terrorism? I'm partly thinking, of course, of the invasion of Iraq.

JA: I think that the conditions under which terrorism can really raise its ugly head are quite varied depending on the context that you are talking about, but one of the causes of terrorism is oppressive Muslim governments. In these countries there's no freedom of expression and dissent, and that becomes a pressure cooker. And unfortunately, Western governments have at different periods been in bed with these Muslim governments and turned a blind eye to the oppression. So many Muslims do not trust the West.

Another major cause is that Western foreign policies, such as the intervention in Iraq, are very misplaced; the invasion of Iraq just made things worse in the Middle East. At one stage also America supported and provided arms to what became Al-Qaeda, and the Taliban in Afghanistan, against the Russians.

RA: You were brought up as a Muslim but you became a Christian in high school, which would have been a difficult move to make. What was so powerful about Christianity that attracted you?

JA: There were a number of things. The first attraction was just the way a Christian friend at school lived his life. He was a genuinely compassionate person, very Godly, very prayerful. I watched him pray and read his scripture in front of me every morning, every evening. It was just compelling. I was brought up with all the stereotypes and prejudices about Christians – they don't pray and they're not to be trusted – and here I was confronted with a completely different model of Christian who didn't fit this image in any way.

RA: And that brings us to the final question about the challenges of Christian-Muslim dialogue. Is the Muslim God the same as the Christian God?

JA: I think that Muslim–Christian dialogue is very essential. We cannot afford not to, it's not an option any longer, we've got to learn to talk to each other and to build bridges.

We don't have to do that, though, by compromising and having theological negotiations and bargaining. I believe that dialogue should be about holding very clearly to our fundamental distinctives; what makes Christianity distinctive and what makes Islam distinctive; we should hold to those differences, but also learn to respect and honour them.

As to whether Muslims and Christians worship the same God, I remember being asked this question back in the mid-'90s by a Christian friend of mine. He asked me, 'When you came to faith in Christ, did you feel like you were switching Gods?' And my instantaneous answer was 'no', I just felt like I was watching an image on black-and-white television and now I'm watching the same image on colour television.

I would rather that my God is the God of the universe, the God of Muslims and Christians, and not a tribal God just for me, just for the Christian tribe. I would rather that people excluded themselves than I exclude them. I would rather my God is an inclusive God.

Understanding and Engaging with Islam

Embracing the 'other' in love, truth and grace

Christians must practise a 'hermeneutic of hospitality' to those who are 'other', including Muslims and non-believers, argues Professor Miroslav Volf, Director of the Centre for Faith and Culture at Yale University. The renowned theologian and author of *Exclusion and Embrace*, one of *Christianity Today*'s 100 best books of the 20th century, spoke to Gordon Preece. Part I of the interview appeared in the May 2014 edition of *TMA*. Part II follows in the next chapter.

GP: Firstly, Miroslav, how has your family formation and racial and religious background as a Croatian in formerly Communist Yugoslavia and as son of a Pentecostal pastor shaped 1. Your own faith, and 2. Your relationship to other faiths?

MV: I was blessed to have three amazing nurturers early in my life, my father, mother, and nanny, all in their own way, saints. Saints with warts, but saints nonetheless. My own faith, and theological articulations of faith, are footnotes to their lived faith. Even when I wasn't particularly close to faith and wanted to rebel it was less because I thought it untrue, or non-genuine, or not beautiful, and more that it was just too hard a burden to bear, the gift too heavy to carry. So my faith journey starts with these extraordinary giants of everyday faith. Their faith was shaped by the utter gratuity of grace, by the consistent and painful practice of forgiveness, and these stances have been the directional push for my theological endeavours.

GP: Can you share about your nanny and parents in relationship to your brother's tragic death?

MV: There was a tragic accident in which my older brother was killed when he was five, because he went to play with "his soldiers", because we lived very close to a small military base. My mother and father were at work, and our nanny was supposed to be caring for us, but she let him slip out to play, and by the negligence of a soldier he was killed. Now my nanny was a true angel of faith, but managing things wasn't really her strong suit. To their credit, my parents not only forgave the soldier but also my nanny. In fact, my mother never spoke an ill word describing the negligence of the nanny for my first 40 years. Forgiven was forgiven and therefore you don't talk about it. I was 42 when I asked my mother, "How come you didn't tell me about it?" and she said, "Well I forgave her, and she stayed with us". Nanny ended up being the angel of my childhood. My first book was dedicated to her because she was such an extraordinary joyful presence in our lives. Yet she was also implicated in some ways, but my parents knew how to forgive and let it go.

GP: So your nanny could still be joyful because she was so freed up by your parent's forgiveness (in more than a merely mental way)? I know you're working on joy these days and I'm wondering about the connection?

MV: The credit is to my parents because they let her be. You could have imagined them constantly bearing down upon her, but she wasn't a simply careless person. It's also a credit to her. She always sang as she went about her duties, and I'm not sure just how she was as joyous as she was. She was a destitute widow, her husband never returned from war, she had no belongings. Yet in the midst of all of this, both with guilt and poverty, she was just a beautiful soul, just wanting to sing and be with the Lord. She is an embodiment of authentic Christian joy and life that isn't artificially generated by a special event, but joy that comes from very deep springs.

GP: You have given lectures about the importance of formative practices like joy in the Christian life, not just abstract world views and systematic theology – though you use all of those. Could you explain how to develop forms of formation for things like joy and forgiveness?

MV: Sure. A world view of things is important but it's like a frame that holds the content. In the intellectual dimensions of Christian faith there is an overarching interpretation of life, but situated within that is an account of the self, of social relations and the good. It's actually the lived life that Christian faith is about. Christian faith is fundamentally about a way of life, but not a blind way of life. That's what was transmitted from my parents and saintly nanny. My job as a theologian is to tease out the ideas embodied in such an incredibly powerful way.

GP: Could you talk about your family's practice of hospitality also, particularly when you were a teen? And how practices like forgiveness, joy, hospitality, work out in relationship to other faiths?

MV: We always had somebody as our guest, either travelling preachers for dad's church, or distant people without a Protestant church. They were assorted characters, not always to my parents' joy, but that's the stuff of which the Christian crowd is made, and their doors of hospitality were open.

One particular guy came once a month for communion. He had this huge Nietzsche-like moustache that hung and stuck out and he would slurp my mother's delicious soup onto it. I was a teenager not keen to be with adults, nor keen about his table noises. It was very off-putting but in retrospect it was an amazing gift to me, the gift of my parents' hospitality. Hospitality given irrespective of people's customs and quirks. It was a lesson in the broader sense of hospitality, of attending to somebody who is different in their difference, without keeping your world so tidy that when they come you feel completely bent out of shape.

We need a kind of 'catholic' or supple sense of identity which can live with the other, standing firm where it stands, but providing space and room to recognise the other in their otherness, including hospitality toward other faiths. Before my father was called to ministry, he worked as a confectioner for a Muslim boss. My dad always used to say, "The best person I ever worked for was this Muslim confectioner." There was high admiration, even while he and his boss were witnessing robustly to each other, with a sense of the rightness of one's own faith. That's an important stance to have to others whether secularists or believers.

GP: You talk in *A Public Faith* about a "hermeneutics of hospitality". How do you see that working out in relation to Muslims?

MV: I formulated it in contrast to "hermeneutics of suspicion", where you seek what is below the surface, something more sinister that they might not even recognise – a kind of "evil eye" looking at the other suspiciously. But a hermeneutics of hospitality, at least as a first step, takes the other as the other presents itself, seeking the good in the other. In the second step there are judgements made, interpreting and assessing. But the first stance is one of openness, reflecting God's basic stance towards humanity, an unconditional love, imitating God's character and action in Christ, reflecting our own justification by sheer grace.

GP: In your most controversial book *Allah*, critics like Dr Mark Durie, an Australian Anglican minister and scholar of Islam, would say, while admiring your loving hospitality towards Muslims, that truth has been compromised. How would you respond to that critique?

MV: Firstly, the hermeneutics of hospitality, which sees the good, isn't contrasted to interest in truth. Truth and love don't stand in opposition, and a hermeneutics of hospitality doesn't relieve you from making correct judgements. And so, to my critics I concede on some points maybe I have been too charitable to some Muslims, but I still have not been persuaded that the critics are right. The book's basic argument, namely that Muslims and Christians, notwithstanding their differences in understanding of God as the Holy Trinity or a simple unity, notwithstanding their differences of understanding Jesus as the self-revelation of God versus prophet; the object of worship is the same, though differently understood.

What I would say to some critics is: "Why is it that in regard to Jews, who have exactly the same and even stronger formulated objections to the doctrines of the Trinity and divinity of Christ, we can, without doubt, say that we worship the same God. But in regard to Muslims who have, content-wise, a very similar understanding of God to the Jews, why are we so hesitant to make that step?" How is that possible and why? I haven't seen an argument for it yet.

GP: Regarding the Jews, the Holocaust produced revisions of Christian theology in repentance for anti-Semitism. But in Christian Muslim relationships, despite the medieval Crusades, there somehow hasn't been a similar process of repentance or dealing with these deep-seated memories, that can be remembered like yesterday. What makes the two sets of relationships, between Christians and Jews and Christians and Muslims, so different now?

MV: That's the right direction for explaining the difference in reactions. In one case, Christians, *en masse*, are the guilty party with regard to the Jews' horrendous persecutions throughout history. In the other case, Christians at least perceive themselves as being on the receiving end of Muslim violence, but that's not how Muslims perceive themselves (as aggressors). I'd hope that whether we are guilty, see ourselves as guilty or as on the receiving end of animosity, we can build bridges to those we have injured as well as to those who have injured us.

GP: How can we get past childish reactions like "You started it?" and the murky mess of history and the blame game?

MV: Christian action shouldn't be reactive. Irrespective of the context or whatever has been done to us, there is a stance that we take which isn't conditioned by others' activity, a kind of non-reactive morality that Christian faith and theology ought to be known by.

GP: Despite some reaction to *Allah*, that you put too much stress on God's love, you started by quoting a Franciscan friend who noted the lack of fear of God on both sides in the Balkans conflict. "Fear of God" is not a popular term these days in modern "soft-bellied" Western Christianity. Where does that enter into the relationship between the religions, and in their self-critique, especially for Christians?

MV: Fear and love of God are like two sides, two dimensions of the same thing. It's love for the sovereignty of the love of God, for the utter claim that God's active love has upon our lives and the holiness of that unconditional love. The utter primacy of that love in our own lives can preserve us from reactive morality – "they did that to us and therefore have to apologise before we make a first step toward them". We are enmeshed in mutually destructive dependence but if we fear God we're taken out of it. We're both secured and compelled by God's love to act the way God does towards God's enemies, which we all, in a profound sense, are.

GP: Your very strong emphasis on forgiveness, reconciliation and embrace comes across as Christian pacifism sometimes, for example in *Exclusion and Embrace*. But you also talk powerfully there about God's judgement against injustice. Along with the fear of God, how does the judgement of God help with issues of conflict reconciliation and justice?

MV: Just as fear of God is the subjective accompaniment of our love for God, so judgement is an accompaniment or dimension of the actuality of God's love, just as the holiness of God is. That is the recognition of the utter primacy and integrity of this love. The human side of that love of God turned toward humans, is both unconditional acceptance and also judgement, a judgement of grace. But judgement is not outside of love, just like I don't think that justice is the opposite to forgiveness, but in every act of forgiveness justice, or "just" claims of one person against another, are both affirmed and transcended. The love of God has justice as part and parcel of it. Injustice cannot be a mode of love, right? So the setting of relationships aright through grace is just what that love is, and that's where God's judgement comes in, judgement against the forms of "unlove", judgement that both condemns, but also calls back and rescues and returns to the good. So we need to talk about the judgement of God. The key question is, how do we understand it?

GP: In *Exclusion and Embrace*, you paraphrased Paul in Romans 12 about leaving vengeance to God. You contrast a university common room setting of abstract academic debate of this issue with the actual genocidal situation taking place, when you were giving the lectures in the Balkans. How does this work out in relation to people who have endured horrendous wrongs?

MV: People who have endured horrendous wrongs want the injustice against them met, and they want the perpetrators of that injustice stopped, they don't want it to happen to others, and they don't want it to happen again to them. They want, ultimately, for the victimiser not to triumph over them, and I think that's the role of God's judgement, and that's also the role of leaving vengeance to God. Exactly how God avenges the wrong, we may debate, but a setting in which a moral order which has been disturbed profoundly by violation of somebody's rights by oppression is reasserted and re-established, that kind of transformative judging and redeeming action of God, is fundamental if there is to be hope for a world of love.

So, judgement and the vengeance of God, and therefore from our side, fear of God, are fundamental in bringing about a world of love. I wouldn't want it otherwise. I wouldn't want anything [evil] that's crawling on the face of the planet now to find its way back to ruin that world of love. So the transformative, purifying judgement of God is a condition of the world of love. In a small way we each experience that when we embrace faith, and when we are given a new birth in baptism we die, and we are raised again as new persons. Each repentance is a form of incarnation of that final judgement, turning away from sin to do righteousness.

....

The Revd Dr Gordon Preece, who was a PhD student of Professor Volf, is the Priest-in-Charge of Yarraville Anglican Parish, Melbourne, Australia; Director of Ethos: EA Centre for Christianity & Society; and Director of the University of Divinity Centre for Research in Religion & Social Policy (RASP).

Understanding and Engaging with Islam

Christianity marginalised if new media ignored

The pace and fragmentation of modern life, family and culture, to say nothing of well-publicised scandals involving religious figures, have made the practice and passing on of religious belief that much more difficult. But Professor Miroslav Volf, Director of the Centre for Faith and Culture at Yale University and renowned author, is an advocate for and practitioner in communicating profound Christian truths in the new media, as he tells Gordon Preece, in the second and final part of an interview which appeared in the June 2014 edition of *TMA*.

GP: You talk in *A Public Faith* about "malformations of faith", and in recent lectures about malformations of faith in the context of globalisation, the processes affecting world religions and media fascination and overexposure. How do those malformations develop in relationship to Christianity and other religions today?

MV: In religion's public and private roles, I've identified two major malfunctions: one is a faith that doesn't shape or direct life, but only comforts and heals. It is malfunctioning because it's not transforming the world in any significant way. The other malfunction is that of coerciveness of faith, a faith that wants to shape the realities but by imposing itself on others.

There is a malfunction of faith which abdicates the notion of truth, that there may be something at stake here in the particular claims Christian faith makes regarding other religions, and therefore gives up witnessing to them. There is also a faith that betrays itself by corrosively and manipulatively imposing itself on others, as if everything different has to be bulldozed away. It can't abide the idea that there may be something we might learn and respect from other faiths, and that therefore we ought to build bridges to them to live in peace with them.

GP: Concerning religious malfunctions, you talk about prophetic types of faith both in public and personal dimensions of faith – everyday, less visible practices. Do these have a prophetic function? I think of your parents' actions, for instance, the things you learnt from them?

MV: I don't like to contrast a private small-scale communal sphere with the public sphere. There are differences, but there has to be integration. What happens in the public domain impacts on a very intimate sphere, even of our desires, and vice versa. What happens in the quiet recesses of the heart, in family rooms and churches, impacts upon the public imagination and how public engagement occurs. The most prophetic thing is a well-lived life, alive in the presence of God. The well of "prophetism" turned outward is a shaping of one's own life in that presence, so this piece of reality I inhabit is conformed to God's transcendent claim, and then speaks consequentially to the wider public. That's not the only way it happens, and sometimes, we as broken people, see things rightly and can project prophetic messages even when unable to live them, but generally our prophetic engagement ought to be nurtured in the deepest recesses of our hearts.

GP: Your first book *Work in the Spirit* enabled Christians to take their work seriously as having some continuity with the new heavens and new earth. In *A Public Faith*, you also talk about the importance of daily work as a form of less glamorous public, prophetic faith. Could you expand on that?

MV: I don't like to contrast church theology and public theology because the church is not only gathered but also in dispersion. When Christians are not gathered around the Lord's Table or around the Word of God or praising God, they are in their workplaces. And it's precisely there that faith has to be lived out, at multiple levels – from private demeanour, the way we look at or relate to another person, to high-level corporate decisions we make. They all ought to reflect deep Christian commitments. Reflection on the nature of human work is an integral aspect of that. Most of our time is spent living Christianly outside of church and home and so we ought to reflect on what it means to live worthy of our calling in those settings.

GP: In *A Public Faith*, you argued against the new atheist assumption that religion is intrinsically violent, contrary to the everyday practices of the great bulk of Christians and other believers. Could you expand on that?

MV: Observing how faiths function in the world, certainly Christian faith, what seems obvious is when there are breakdowns and hypocrisies, particularly of relatively prominent people. It can sensitise us to possible dangers or breakdowns of our own faith, but we shouldn't confuse the media prevalence of such events with the reality of ordinary people's lives. Regular worship and faith can function as a very sturdy spiritual capital in our everyday practices. Instead of simply zeroing in on egregious cases, we ought to attend to how faith functions most broadly, without wanting to separate ourselves from people who commit egregious acts.

GP: Recent surveys by and of, for example, a megachurch like Willow Creek or the UK Evangelical Alliance note a massive deficit of discipling practices, particularly for younger people. How is your Centre for Faith and Culture at Yale tackling these issues?

MV: It's a huge challenge. Part of the reason for our program on Adolescent Faith and Flourishing is because we want to attend to the transmission of faith understood as not just beliefs but as an integral set of practices, especially in adolescence. The person running this program is one of the rare senior ministers, especially of a wealthy and prominent congregation, who has made his top priority to attend to and be with adolescents. It's gone from a very small group to one of the most well-known youth programs in the city. We need to pay much more attention to that liminal stage, especially as often in homes, the faith is not transmitted anymore in traditional ways, partly because of a breakdown of sturdy, continuous, stable family life.

GP: In talking with a group of Christian professionals in India recently, a female architect raised the issue of time pressure and fragmentation making it difficult to have practices like praying and reading Scripture as it's hard enough now to get families together for a meal. Can some of the practices of your Croatian context, which stamped your character and discipleship, be translated into a different Western context today?

MV: In many ways, I don't have even beginnings of an answer. One of the great challenges in our modern globalised way of life, in being always connected and wired, is the difficulty of transmitting traditional cultural and religious words and practices. How does transmission happen? Our ethnic customs, eating practices, religious celebrations, all take time and repetition. They take on the stable continuity of interactions, and in a ritualised form, but that has become increasingly difficult in a globalised age where our attention is completely divided and we're dispersed. You can't get a family to sit around the common table, it's a huge cultural challenge, but also for transmission of faith and the shaping of influences, so you can observe how faith works in people's lives and has lasting impact on your life. That's a great challenge that we need to devote real energy to figure out.

GP: For all your trying to pass on Christian cultural practices, you're also strongly engaged with various media: you tweet, you've got over 10,000 Facebook followers, you were on the ABC's Q&A. You talked earlier about being in an age that finds it difficult to do abstract theological or philosophical reasoning, and that you've adapted your own patterns of writing and communication. For all the profound classical theology below the tip of the iceberg, you write with increasing simplicity, in a publicly accessible way, though dealing with difficult issues. How do you do it?

MV: Unless theologians and church folk learn first how to connect the central claims and convictions of Christian faith with the central challenges of life so faith becomes alive, we'll marginalise ourselves. While scholarly theological research is essential, ways of communicating are needed for people untrained to follow 200 pages of an argument, but who live in a very impressionistic, quick quip-like, aphoristic kind of culture, with images combined with narratives.

We need to communicate profound Christian truths and concerns in new media. So I try to tie Christian convictions to particular stories and narratives of life. On Twitter, I use aphorisms, which is an intellectual achievement if done well. Great aphorists like Nietzsche compress amazing amounts of thought that stimulates thinking, opening up possibilities. Twitter can be very trite but it creates possibilities for very reflective engagement. That's at least what I'm trying to do with social media.

The Revd Dr Gordon Preece, who was a PhD student of Professor Volf, is the Priest-in-Charge of Yarraville Anglican Parish, Melbourne, Australia; Director of Ethos: EA Centre for Christianity & Society; and Director of the University of Divinity Centre for Research in Religion & Social Policy (RASP).

Understanding and Engaging with Islam

Church called to go out onto the 'field of battle'

The Church should operate like a field hospital after battle, binding up wounds, says William T. Cavanaugh, borrowing a metaphor used by Pope Francis. Author of numerous books and a professor of theology at DePaul University in Chicago, Dr Cavanaugh spoke to Roland Ashby following his address to an international colloquium on religion and violence. The article appeared in the August 2016 edition of *TMA*.

The only thing that will save the world, according to René Girard, is "to adopt the behaviour recommended by Christ: abstain completely from retaliation, and renounce the escalation to extremes".

William Cavanaugh likes this quote from the French philosopher and theorist on the causes of violence because for him it goes both to the heart of the Christian message and why he is a Christian. "It explains for me why Christianity is not just useful or beautiful, but true."

For him Girard makes sense of the Christian claim that Jesus Christ saved the world, "and Christ saves the world by undoing the cycle of violence that is so prevalent… God comes to earth, we kill him and God doesn't retaliate".

Imagine the effect, he says, if Christians were to put this non-retaliation into practice. "Never mind pacifism, consider the impact if we started to take Just War theory seriously. If large numbers of Christians in the US military had decided that the war with Iraq was not a Just War, and refused to fight, the effect would have been revolutionary."

But in response to the new atheists' argument that religion is to blame for the world's violence, he says there is a level playing field between the religious and secular on this matter and that secular society is capable of being just as violent as religious groups.

"By invading Iraq the idea of course was to make it more reasonable and secular and rational, and that was going to bring peace, but of course that's based on the idea that when we kill people it doesn't really count as violence. It's violence if you detonate bombs in backpacks, but it's not violence if you drop bombs from 30,000 feet."

He says secular societies in the West have increasingly used religion as a scapegoat over violence. "That's what secular societies in the West tend to be based on; this idea that we've been saved from the chaos that religion causes by marginalising religion in public life and pushing if off to a kind of poorly organised leisure activity on Sunday morning."

But just as religious people kill others because of idolatry – the creation and worship of a false god – so secular people also kill because of idolatry, "of things like money and flags and oil and freedom that function as gods in people's lives", he writes in his latest book *Field Hospital – the church's engagement with a wounded world.*

Secular society, he says, has replaced God with the idolatrous worship of money and the economy, something which has led to economic and political wounds, and wounds from violence — a theme he explores in *Field Hospital.*

The economic and political wounds, he says, can be seen in the "exploitation and marginalisation of people, the expansion of inequality, the way that people are mesmerised by consumer products, and the manipulation of people's desires". He believes marginalisation and the growing divide between rich and poor also largely explain the popularity of Donald Trump and Bernie Saunders in the US, and the Brexit vote in Britain.

"Money has replaced God in our culture, as Philip Goodchild argues in his book *The Theology of Money*, and I agree with Robert H. Nelson that modern economics offers its own worldview which stands in sharp contrast to the Christian worldview. Economics used to be a branch of moral theology, but now it is geared towards econometrics and what is quantifiable, and embedded within it is a whole series of assumptions about the nature of the human person. It has replaced God with a different measure of value, which is money."

The dangerous and corrosive view of people that economics is fostering, he believes, is that "we are essentially consuming beings who pursue our own interests, and those interests might include the interests of others, but they might not". "Another assumption is the idea that we're all individuals, and so we interact in the marketplace as individuals, not as social creatures, which I think is just false."

He believes a fundamental problem for humanity, particularly in our post-Christendom West, is symbolised in The Fall, which in *Field Hospital* he argues was about falsely imagining that freedom means being free from God, and that we are the source of our own being. Any attempt to escape dependence on God and interdependence with other people is fruitless, he writes, and it is self-deceptive to live as though one were self-sufficient.

Modernity, he says, is in many ways "typified by the replacement of the good with freedom as the goal of life". "But this brings certain distortions including the view of the self as free, autonomous consumer, where we stand back from everything, including God, and make our choices.

"But in reality we are enmeshed in relationships with other people from the day we're born, and we're also enmeshed ultimately in a relationship with God."

This also brings responsibilities to care for other people, particularly when they're at their most vulnerable, as in the parable of The Good Samaritan. "In The Good Samaritan, the original Greek means that the Samaritan is 'moved in his gut'; his response was a gut reaction of flesh calling out to flesh, and there's that really personal dimension that I think Pope Francis has a good sense of, that you need to have personal contact with people who suffer. That's what the Gospel is calling us to – something that has been largely lost in our abstract, bureaucratised and institutionalised society.

"We now think that our Christian duty is done if we pay our taxes to support the welfare state, and we expect the state to take care of people, and we're not willing to enter into the sort of risk that's involved in personal relationships.

"The whole idea of personalism is that you don't leave it to the state to do it, but you have an encounter involving personal sacrifice. This is why the Incarnation is important. This is why God became flesh – so that we might encounter God in the flesh and not leave it to a kind of abstraction that separates us from one another."

He writes in *Field Hospital* that when Pope Francis was asked by a journalist "What kind of Church do you dream of?" he replied, "The thing the Church needs most today is the ability to heal wounds... I see the Church as a field hospital after battle".

Professor Cavanaugh's dream for the Church is that it should integrate worship, devotion and social activism. "I think of someone like Dorothy Day for whom the daily Eucharist was essential to her activism. For her it was as essential to see Christ in the poor who came to her door each day as it was to see and receive Christ each day in the Eucharist.

"The Church I dream of is about seeing each other as all inherently related to one another because we're all children of the same God, and learning to see the world from a God's eye view where national boundaries are artificial.

"And it's about being a Church that is not just a hospital, but a *field* hospital

– a mobile place which goes out rather than waits for people to come to it, and is willing to go out onto the field of battle and take risks."

Appendix

Understanding Pope Francis' spirituality

Pope Francis demonstrably has a deep love for God and people, and often seems to incarnate the love and grace of Christ, something which lies at the heart of his spiritual formation as a Jesuit. Roland Ashby reflects on the life-changing nature of the Spiritual Exercises of Spanish mystic St Ignatius of Loyola, who founded the Jesuit order in 1539 and whose Exercises are at the core of Ignatian spirituality.

Would you like God to convert you, change you and transform you utterly in love? This was the question on the flyer to promote a retreat entitled "Transformed Utterly in Love", an introduction to St Ignatius' Spiritual Exercises at the Campion Centre of Ignatian Spirituality in Melbourne, Australia.

How could I possibly resist the offer to be "transformed utterly in love"? I thought, eagerly signing up. And after completing this introductory retreat, I decided to go further – immersing myself in the Exercises over a 30-week period under the guidance of a spiritual director, who I met weekly for the duration.

Jesuits are normally required to complete the Exercises in a retreat of 30 days, but completing them "part-time" over 30 weeks is another option, particularly for lay people who are working.

This "30 weeks in daily life retreat" also seeks to integrate the Exercises into normal daily life, and covers the same material as the 30-day retreat, which is divided into four weeks or segments: God's love for us despite our sinfulness; Christ's life and ministry; Christ's Passion and Death; and finally, the Resurrection and life in the Spirit.

Being transformed utterly in love was a process that began for St Ignatius when he was recovering from severe injuries sustained in battle. For this dashing young man – something of an Errol Flynn or Brad Pitt type perhaps, with an eye for the ladies and the main chance, and with dreams of fame and glory as a soldier – life was to change dramatically when a cannon ball shattered one of his legs; and in the long recovery period he read about the lives of the saints, and found they inspired him in a way that his military heroes could not.

So began a lifelong and life-changing love affair which would lead him to offer his life in the complete love and service of Christ, and he was able to pray:

Take Lord, and receive all my liberty,
My memory, my understanding,
and my entire will,
All that I have and possess.
You have given all to me.
To you, Lord, I return it.
All is yours.
Dispose of it according to your will.
Give me your love and grace,
For this is sufficient for me.

He also wrote: "There are very few who realise what God would make of them if they abandoned themselves entirely into His hands, and let themselves be formed by His Grace."

The idea of falling in love with God and Christ was explored by St Ignatius' 20th century successor as Superior General of the Jesuits, Fr Pedro Arrupe, who wrote that:

"Nothing is more practical than finding God, than falling in Love in a quite absolute, final way… Fall in Love, stay in love, and it will decide everything."

So what are the practicalities of finding God, and "falling in love in a quite absolute, final way" for the Jesuit?

They include what Ignatius called the **Principle and Foundation**: recognising that I am created by the God who is love, to love, praise and serve God – "I am from love, of love, for love", as one translation puts it.

The Daily Examen at the end of each day, which invites you to reflect on how God has loved you, and to give thanks for the many blessings and graces you have received throughout the day.

As part of the Examen, **The Discernment of Spirits** includes seeking to discern where you have been loving and generous-hearted; and also where you have failed to love, or have been stony-hearted.

The Imaginative Contemplation, which invites you to place yourself in a Gospel scene as either an observer or as one of the protagonists, imagining the sights, sounds and smells so that you feel physically present, and ending with a colloquy, or conversation, with Christ.

I found this way of engaging with Scripture particularly powerful. One of my journal entries reads:

"The Imaginative Contemplations have helped me to experience the physical presence of Christ, to feel his touch and embrace when being held in his arms as one of the children he blesses; to feel his hand holding mine when I was the blind man he led out of the city. Imagining myself as Simeon, I have also experienced the joy of holding him as an infant.

"Through the Imaginative Contemplations I have been physically present to witness Christ's great and healing love for others, and its transforming effects on them."

Falling in love with Christ is also about experiencing the power of forgiveness – for oneself and for others. It is difficult to love and forgive – yourself and others – unless you have experienced being loved and forgiven. Jesus said of Mary of Bethany, the "sinful woman" who showed him great love by anointing his feet with perfume and washing them with her hair, that "he who has been forgiven little, loves little" (see Luke 7: 36-50).

The second great commandment – "love others as yourself" – is difficult unless we know and experience God's love for us, despite our sinfulness. This is the love which has enabled Jean Vanier, the founder of the L'Arche Communities for the disabled, to say, "Each of us is more beautiful than we can dare to believe [because we] are children of God". God has an enormous love for us, writes poet Edwina Gateley, and all he wants to do is to "look upon [us] with that love".

One of the most painful, but cathartic and liberating, moments of the 30 weeks came for me when my director suggested I write an apology to someone I had wronged nearly 40 years ago, and then to give the matter up to Christ. Learning to let go of past mistakes, and see them as "buried in the heart of Christ", as Br Roger of Taize put it, is a critical part of learning to love and forgive – yourself and others.

The Spirit-filled ministry of Pope Francis, who has acknowledged the failures of his early priestly ministry, is testament to the power of such forgiveness, and to the love that "transforms utterly".

www.ingramcontent.com/pod-product-compliance
Lightning Source LLC
Chambersburg PA
CBHW070153100426
42743CB00013B/2898